Jerky Recipes

The Ultimate Guide to Drying and Preserving Meat, Fish, Fowl, and More through Traditional Methods

© **Copyright 2024 - All rights reserved.**

The content contained within this book may not be reproduced, duplicated, or transmitted without direct written permission from the author or the publisher.

Under no circumstances will any blame or legal responsibility be held against the publisher or author for any damages, reparation, or monetary loss due to the information contained within this book, either directly or indirectly.

Legal Notice:

This book is copyright-protected. It is only for personal use. You cannot amend, distribute, sell, use, quote, or paraphrase any part of the content within this book without the consent of the author or publisher.

Disclaimer Notice:

Please note the information contained within this document is for educational and entertainment purposes only. All effort has been executed to present accurate, up-to-date, reliable, and complete information. No warranties of any kind are declared or implied. Readers acknowledge that the author is not engaging in the rendering of legal, financial, medical, or professional advice. The content within this book has been derived from various sources. Please consult a licensed professional before attempting any techniques outlined in this book.

By reading this document, the reader agrees that under no circumstances is the author responsible for any losses, direct or indirect, that are incurred as a result of the use of the information contained within this document, including, but not limited to, errors, omissions, or inaccuracies.

Table of Contents

Introduction 1

Chapter 1: Introduction to Making Jerky 3

Chapter 2: Choosing the Right Meat
and Ingredients 15

Chapter 3: Jerky Preparation Techniques 30

Chapter 4: Dehydrating and Smoking
Jerky 42

Chapter 5: Jerky Recipes for Different
Proteins 56

Chapter 6: Flavorful Jerky Marinades
and Seasonings 119

Chapter 7: Storing and Packaging Jerky 151

Chapter 8: Exploring Jerky Culture and
Innovations 158

Conclusion 169

References 171

Introduction

There's no better snack in the world than a piece of jerky. It is delicious, an incredibly healthy food to snack on, and contains none of those empty calories that come from other snacks, like chips and candy. Every bite of jerky is packed with nutrients that feed your body.

So why should you make your own jerky? Why not just buy it?

It's quite simple, really. Not only is store-bought jerky expensive, but it is also likely to be full of unhealthy additives. When you make it yourself, you know exactly what goes into it – whole, healthy ingredients.

By the time you get to the end of this guide, you'll be making healthy, tasty jerky with ease, and you'll never look at store-bought options again. And there's no limit to what you can turn into jerky. It's not just beef. You can use chicken, turkey, duck, goose, lamb, pork, and rabbit. You can even use bear, crocodile, ostrich, and any other meat you can think of. And if you don't eat meat, it's not a problem – plenty of vegetables can be turned into jerky and protein sources, such as soy and tempeh, so no one is left out of this wonderful experience.

How to Use This Book

This book is packed with useful information on making and storing jerky, including tons of recipes for different jerky and marinades to give them an extra boost of flavor and nutrition. Don't be scared to try this. If you follow a few simple tips and have the right equipment, making jerky is so simple that you'll always make it.

If you are new to making jerky, start with the simpler recipes. When you have perfected those, you can move on to more complex marinades and different cuts of meat before you finally get creative and create your own unique, delicious recipes.

Food Safety

One thing you must keep in mind is safety. When working with meat and fish, always handle them carefully, as poorly handled food can be a source of foodborne illnesses. All food has its own requirements, so do your research before you start. Meat should be heated to at least 160°F for half an hour or more to kill off any potentially dangerous bacteria.

Other than that, follow the recipe and storage directions carefully, and you'll have safe, healthy jerky to eat whenever you want it.

This book is simple to follow, with plenty of step-by-step directions, so let's not waste any more time. Dive right in and start making delicious jerky today.

Chapter 1: Introduction to Making Jerky

There is nothing complicated about jerky. It is simply meat, poultry, game, or even vegetables marinated in certain seasonings and spices and then dried in thin strips. It is one of the most delicious, flavorful, and healthy snacks of all time, and its origins go a long way back.

1. There is nothing complicated about jerky. Source: https://unsplash.com/photos/a-white-plate-topped-with-fried-food-on-top-of-a-table-h7UpTT95Bh4?utm_content=creditShareLink&utm_medium=referral&utm_source=unsplash

The Fascinating Jerky Journey

Jerky has been a food staple for thousands of years, and the earliest forms can be traced to ancient Egyptian times. During those early days, meat was preserved in various ways to ensure food was available when crops and other food sources were in short supply. However, it was in Peru that the closest thing to modern jerky was found in the Andes mountains, where indigenous communities thrived.

Worldwide, cultures have been preserving meat in many ways to help provide long-term food supplies. When you dry meat and fish, you get a low-fat, high-protein snack packed with nutrition, and when you add dried veggies to that, you have all the nutrition you need. Aside from being used as food supplies when other sources are scarce, jerky also makes a great snack.

Who Invented Jerky?

The first jerky, and still the most popular today, was beef. Modern-day beef jerky was first invented in Peru when the indigenous communities in the Andes made it to preserve meat when supplies were high for times when they were low. The Andes mountains have a unique high-altitude climate, perfect for making and storing the jerky long-term. We can thank the Quechua tribe from South America for the word "jerky." Their preserved meat was named "Ch'arki," which means "to burn meat."

The tribes set strips of meat out to dry in the sun during the day and allowed it to freeze when the nights were colder. Today, the jerky we make or buy is pure meat, but in those days, it would have had bones in it. It also wasn't always made from beef. Other meats used were guanacos, llamas, alpacas, vicuna, and other Camelidae animals, all commonly found roaming the area at the time.

Day-time drying and night-time freezing had a few advantages, and the main one was that large amounts of meat could be dried at the same time. Every year, around 15% of each animal herd was slaughtered to produce meat for consumption, and a high percentage of that was used to make Ch'arki, ensuring the tribe had enough food to last the whole year.

When the Spanish conquistadors arrived in the New World, the word Ch'arki became charqui, and from there, it began its evolution into what we know as beef jerky today.

When Was It Invented?

We can trace jerky back much further than modern-day Peru. The earliest forms of Ch'arki can be traced back to the 1550s, but even earlier records indicate that meat was preserved in ancient Egyptian times by drying it in the sun. Preserving food was important to the Egyptians and this can be seen by the sheer amount of preserved food and drink items found in tombs, some of it more intact than others.

Is Jerky Native American?

It is widely believed that jerky originated with the Native Americans, and yes, early tribes did make some kinds of jerky. However, their versions of jerky were not pure meat as we expect today. Rather, they were a combination of fat, ground berries, and fat, made into small cakes called Pemmican. These were packed with protein and nutrients and could be stored safely for long periods.

These cakes ensured the tribes could survive the bitter winters, and they taught their methods to early settlers who adopted their methods.

Many North American tribes also used a different method of preservation – smoking. Each tribe had its own method of smoking, from small enclosed places to large open fires. Traditionally, these tribes would use smoke sheds or big tipis to smoke a lot of meat at the same time.

Wild game was the most used form of protein for jerky, but bison or buffalo were also used on occasion. Fish was a big part of the Northwestern tribal diet, and much of what they caught every year would be made into jerky to see them though leaner times of the year. So, while jerky was certainly not a Native American invention, there is no denying that the methods they used to smoke meat have and continue to play an important role in what we know as jerky today.

Fun Fact: The first use of the word "jerky" in the written language dates back to 1612. It was found on a map of Virginia by John Smith, where he wrote the following: *"as drie as their jerkin beefe in the West Indies."*

How Cowboys Made Jerky

Cowboys were once called "cow hunters," and, in the 1820s, when they moved their cattle about, they would take salted beef with them to sustain them on the long journey. They used many methods to dry their meat, but the most popular techniques were sun-drying, smoking, and salting.

2. Cowboys were once called "cow hunters." Source: https://unsplash.com/photos/brown-and-white-cow-on-green-grass-field-during-daytime-eGFmwUY2oAg?utm_content=creditShareLink&utm_medium=referral&utm_source=unsplash

Cowboys would slaughter whatever meat was available – bison, elk, cattle, antelope, and deer – and cut the meat into thin strips. They would then salt, smoke, or dry it and store it for the long term. Traditional "cowboy" jerky can still be bought today, and it is incredibly delicious but drier and tougher than modern jerky, taking longer to chew and lasting longer.

Most Americans believe that the only jerky is beef jerky, and it is certainly one of the best-selling forms of jerky across the country. That said, there are many different meats that can be turned into jerky:

- Yak
- Wild turkey
- Wild sheep

- Rhea
- Reindeer
- Rabbit
- Pronghorn
- Pheasant
- Ostrich
- Mutton
- Muskrat
- Muskoxen
- Mountain lion
- Mountain goat
- Moose
- Llama
- Kangaroo
- Goose
- Fish
- Elk
- Deer
- Camel
- Bison
- Beaver
- Alligator

And lots more.

Hikers and travelers the world over carry jerky with them when they set out on their travels, and making it at home couldn't be easier. Before diving into making your own jerky, you need to understand food safety.

Food Safety

Making jerky is fun, but unless you follow a few simple rules, it may not be safe to eat:

1. **Make Sure Your Kitchen Is Spotless**. Wipe down all the sides, and clean all the utensils and any other equipment using a weak bleach solution in hot water. Before you start, wash your hands using soap and hot water.

2. **Frozen Meat Must Be Thawed in the Refrigerator**. Not out in the open at room temperature. This ensures bacteria cannot grow. Too many people leave a chunk of meat on the kitchen counter to thaw, but this is unsafe and should never be done. Remove your meat from the freezer the day before you want to make the jerky, and place it in your refrigerator.

3. **Meat Should Be Marinated at 36 to 40°F**. Meat should never be left at room temperature to marinate unless the recipe specifically states it; make sure your meat stays in the refrigerator until you are ready to marinate it, and once placed in the marinade, it must go back in the refrigerator. Raw meat is a great host for bacteria, especially when left out at room temperature. Once you have marinated your meat, discard the marinade. Do **NOT** use it on other meat, as it can cause cross-contamination and increase bacterial growth.

4. **Heat Jerky to 160°F if You Are Using a Dehydrator.** This should be done at the start of the drying process, and it helps kill off harmful bacteria in the meat. When making poultry jerky, it should be heated to 165°F before dehydrating. When you dehydrate meat, it turns heat-resistant, so if you wait until after you have dehydrated it, the heat will not kill all the bacteria. That said, some modern dehydrators have a setting that will heat the meat to 165°F – if yours does, you can forget the preheating and jump straight to dehydrating. If not, marinate the meat, heat it, and then dehydrate it. It is always safer to preheat poultry regardless, just to make sure it can be safely consumed.

5. **Use Curing Salt.** This will help prevent bacterial growth. Using the right amount of curing salt will not cause the harm claimed by those who say salt is dangerous. However, if you opt not to use salt, you must ensure all other safety precautions are followed. A salt cure is advisable if you are making jerky from ground meat. Ground meat has already been handled during several different processes, which makes it more likely to contain harmful bacteria.

6. **Store It Properly.** It can be stored somewhere cool and dark for up to one week or frozen for up to six months.

Preparing the Meat

While making jerky is actually quite easy, the hardest part is to cut the meat into the long, thin strips you need. Fresh meat is usually soft and pliable, so the easiest way to do this is to freeze it before you slice it. You don't need to freeze it solid, just enough to harden it up to make cutting easier.

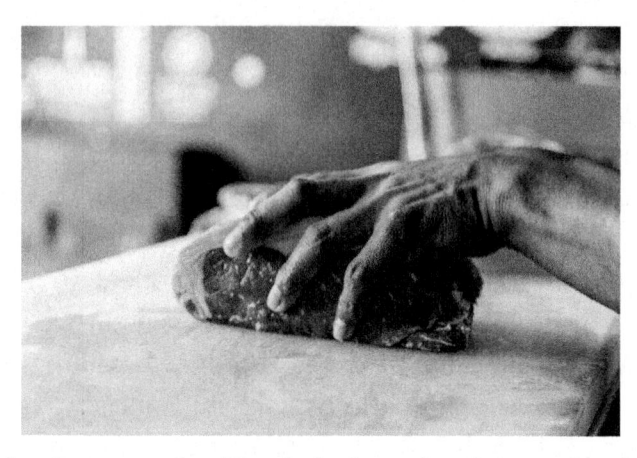

3. *The hardest part of making jerky is cutting the meat into long, thin strips. Source: https://unsplash.com/photos/a-butcher-holding-a-piece-of-meat-in-his-hand-in-boca-del-rio-XpmsZmAMf_g?utm_content=creditShareLink&utm_medium=referral&utm_source=unsplash*

Don't forget to trim off the fat before you prepare your meat. Good jerky is made with lean meat – too much fat stops it from drying out and turns it into a greasy mess. On top of that, fat goes off quickly, and your jerky won't smell good as it dries.

How you cut it depends entirely on how you like jerky. Cut along the grain for chewy meat and across the grain for more tender jerky. However you slice it, it should not be any more than 1 to 1 ½ inches wide and ¼-inch thick. If you can keep your strips as evenly sized as possible, they will dry evenly.

Once you have cut your meat into strips, you have two choices: dry it straight away or marinate it to add flavor and tenderize it. A marinade should contain an acid (lemon juice, vinegar, etc.) and whatever seasonings you want, and the food should be marinated in the refrigerator.

When you make jerky from ground meat, you should mix the meat with a curing mix and dry spice rather than a wet marinade.

How to Destroy Microorganisms

When you dry your meat using an oven or dehydrator, the temperatures are insufficient to destroy microorganisms usually found in raw meat. Although your jerky may look ready to eat when it is done, another step is required to make sure it is safe. While this should be done before drying, it is possible to do it afterward.

- **Pre-Cook:** The USDA Meat and Poultry Hotline strongly recommends pre-cooking your meat. It won't take as long to dry but don't expect it to feel or look the same as traditional jerky. First, slice the meat, then marinade it for however long the recipe recommends. It should then be laid out on trays, evenly spaced, and heated to 160°F in an oven (poultry should be 165°F.) Another way of doing it is to put the meat and marinade in a large pan and heat it until it is simmering. However, the internal temperatures still have to be 160 or 165°F, no matter how you do it.

- **Post-Dry**: Once the jerky has been dried, lay the strips on a baking sheet. Make sure they do not touch or overlap. Your oven should be preheated to 275°F, and the strips should be cooked for 10 minutes. Use a food thermometer to check the temperature. If the meat or poultry has not reached

160°F or 165°F respectively, continue heating for a few minutes and check again.

Drying Meat

While you can sun-dry your meat, the best options are dehydrating or oven-drying.

- **Oven-Drying**: Maintain a low temperature in your oven, 140 to 175°F. You also need good airflow, so leave the oven door open slightly and stand a fan facing the oven. This helps the heat circulate evenly and also helps remove moisture that comes from the drying meat.

- **Dehydrator**: You can't just chuck your meat into an electric dehydrator and switch it on. First, you need to know the temperature it operates at when there's nothing in it. You certainly mustn't accept the temperature controls for what they say because there's every chance they are not accurate. Here's how to find out its operating temperature:
    - Dehydrators with rear fans tend to have a horizontal airflow. In this case, simply shut a food thermometer inside the dehydrator.
    - Dehydrators with bottom or top fans have a vertical airflow. In this case, put three dehydrator trays on the base and insert the stem of a food thermometer in between the top ones. Make sure the dial is on the outside of the unit and place the cover on.
    - Turn your dehydrator to its hottest temperature and switch it on.

- o Wait a few minutes. When the dehydrator temperature has steadied, record it. Do this for all the different temperature settings.
- o If you don't have a choice of temperature settings on your machine, see if you change the ventilation level up or down. This helps let heat out or keep it in to change the temperature.
- o For a dehydrator to be safe for making jerky, it must reach at least 145°F.

Chapter 2: Choosing the Right Meat and Ingredients

The best jerky is only as good as the ingredients you use to make it. Use poor cuts of meat, poultry, or fish, or poor marinade seasonings, and the end product won't be great. This chapter will walk you through tips on making truly great jerky, including the best cuts of meat, poultry, fish, and other products, marinading tips, and sourcing the best products.

4. Jerky is only as good as the ingredients you use to make it. Source: Severein, CC0, via Wikimedia Commons: https://commons.wikimedia.org/wiki/File:Beef-jerky.jpg

Making the Best Jerky

All recipes rely on the right ingredients, and jerky is no different. This chapter starts with a few tips on how to make the best jerky:

1. Choose the Right Meat

Virtually all meat can be dried into jerky, but you must consider that when you dehydrate meat, the flavors become more concentrated and intense. Let's say you have a piece of raw inner loin. While it was being field-dressed, a bit of gut juice spilled on it. No, that's not a nice thought, but it happens. When you dry that piece of meat, it is going to smell. So, overall quality and freshness are critical when making great jerky.

Fat is also an issue. While beef, pork, or lamb fat can provide great flavor to meat, not all fats are equal – for example, deer fat is not so great in the flavor stakes. Apart from that, fat has a lot of water in it, so drying fatty meat takes much longer and often doesn't dry very evenly. And because fat goes off quicker than meat, jerky made from fatty meat will go off quicker than jerky made with lean meat.

Lean meat is always the best choice for jerky, especially wild game meat, as it has little intramuscular fat. Other cuts that work are large ones that you can slice into strips. For example, the backstrap is great for jerky, and apart from the slicing, it needs very little work. Because cuts from the hindquarters of beef cattle are commonly used in making high-quality jerky, you can also get away with using the hindquarters from moose, elk, or deer.

2. Grind or Cut Your Meat

Muscle meat has a grain running through it, with muscle fibers running relatively uniformly. When you cut against that grain, i.e., perpendicular to it, you get a tender, softer jerky. Cutting with the grain makes a stringy, tough jerky, so, where possible, always cut against the grain.

It is recommended to slice your meat into 1/8 to ¼-inch thick strips – the thinner it is, the better the jerky. You should also freeze the meat for one or two hours first, making cutting it exactly as you want easier.

If your budget doesn't stretch to premium cuts, use a lower-quality meat and make it into a ground jerky. Take all the fat and silver skin from the meat, and use a meat grinder with the smallest grinder plate to grind the meat down. Run the meat through twice so you have a fine burger-meat consistency. Shape your ground meat, cure it, and dry it.

3. Use an Effective Method for Drying

While there are several methods of drying, there are three that truly work to help you make the best jerky:

- **Oven-Drying:** This is by far the simplest method. Once your strips have been marinated, put them on an oven rack, evenly spaced. Then, put your oven on its lowest temperature and let the meat dry. If the lowest temperature on your oven is over 160°F, prop the oven door open just a little, enough to allow some of the heat to escape.

- **Dehydrating:** The same principle applies here, as a dehydrator is nothing more than a fan-assisted electric oven. The dehydrator temperature should be between 135 and 165°F, and the meat should reach 160°F inside when done, or 165°F if it is poultry, as those temperatures will kill off E. coli and salmonella bacteria.

5. *A dehydrator can help you make the best jerky. Source: Karelj, Public domain, via Wikimedia Commons: https://commons.wikimedia.org/wiki/File:Drying_owen_1.jpg*

- **Smoking:** This adds great flavor and is very easy, especially if a pellet smoker is used. Check the manufacturer's instructions for your smoker, but it should have a "keep warm" setting that stays at around 165°F. ¼-inch thick strips typically take at least 10 hours in a smoker with an ice tray, around 4 hours without the ice tray or a dehydrator, and up to three hours in an oven.

Knowing when the jerky is done is the hardest part, as it has to be gauged by how it feels, not by cooking time. When you pick up a piece of dried jerky, it should be soft enough to be torn rather than breaking but firm enough not to flop over.

4. **Store the Jerky:** As soon as the jerky is finished, stop the process. Lift the jerky off the rack, pop it in a

resealable bag, seal it, and hold it under cold running water as cold as possible. Then you can refrigerate it. This takes the heat out of the jerky, so it won't dry any further. If it is allowed to carry on drying, it will become tough and almost inedible. Once the jerky has cooled right down, store it in a container with a lid, but not an airtight container, as this just encourages mold to form. You also need to ensure the jerky strips are spaced out and not packed in a tight bundle, as this can lead to mold. Refrigerate it if you don't expect to eat it all within a week. Longer than two weeks, and it has to be stored in the freezer.

The Right Cuts

If you are serious about making homemade jerky, getting the best cuts of meat, poultry, or fish is critical. Here's what you need:

Beef

These are the eight main parts:

6. *Brisket is one of the main eight parts of beef. Source: Pannet, CC BY-SA 4.0 <https://creativecommons.org/licenses/by-sa/4.0>, via Wikimedia Commons: https://commons.wikimedia.org/wiki/File:%D0%93%D0%BE%D0 %B2%D1%8F%D0%B6%D1%8C%D1%8F_%D0%B3%D1%80%D1%8 3%D0%B4%D0%B8%D0%BD%D0%BA%D0%B0.jpg*

1. Brisket
2. Chuck rib
3. Flank
4. Fore shank
5. Round or topside
6. Short loin
7. Short plate
8. Sirloin

These are known as the prime cuts, while sub-primal or smaller cuts come from these. It's easy to see how you could get confused and not know what cut to choose, but some are better suited to jerky.

Eye of Round:

The most popular cut for jerky is an oval muscle located in the cow's hind legs. It makes great jerky because:

- It is lean.
- There is little fat.
- The grain runs the entire length, making it easy to cut.
- It is a cheaper cut of meat.

The Bottom Round:

The outermost muscle at the top of the rear leg is another great choice for jerky, even though it isn't the tenderest cut.

- It is lean.
- It has a marbling effect on its interior.
- It isn't expensive.

- It has great flavor.

Top Round or Topside:

A similar texture to the bottom round, top round, or topside comes the muscle on the inner leg – the opposite side to the bottom round. It isn't as tender as the eye of the round but is more tender than the bottom round.

- It is lean.
- It has less fat.
- It has great flavor.
- It's an economical cut.

Sirloin Tip:

One of the most tender cuts of beef, it isn't the most popular for jerky but is still a great cut.

- It is incredibly lean.
- It is one of the most tender.
- It isn't a cheap cut.

Flank Steak:

You will get great, tender jerky if you slice the flank steak against the grain. Slice it with the grain, and you'll get tough jerky.

- It is lean, but some fat will need to be trimmed off.
- It has a lot of interior marbling.
- It can produce tough jerky.
- It is quite expensive.

Fish

Several fish varieties have been used to make jerky, each with its own characteristics and flavor profiles. These are the best:

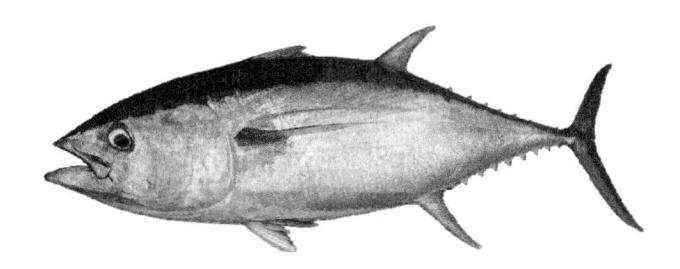

7. *Ahi is a popular choice of fish for making jerky. Source: SEFSC Pascagoula Laboratory; Collection of Brandi Noble, NOAA/NMFS/SEFSC., Public domain, via Wikimedia Commons: https://commons.wikimedia.org/wiki/File:Yellowfin-transp.png*

- **Ahi:** One of the more popular choices of fish for making jerky, tuna has a rich flavor and a beautiful red color. It is moderate in fat and can retain moisture while making a wonderfully chewy texture.
- **Rainbow Trout:** Produces a delicious jerky with a subtle, nutty flavor. Because it is lean, it dries well, producing a highly flavored, tender jerky.
- **Cod:** A delicately flavored flaky white fish, cod is lean, making it great for jerky.
- **Perch:** Another lean choice, perch is mild and a little sweet. Because it is a small fish, it makes great bite-sized jerky snacks.
- **Pickerel and Pike:** These are freshwater fish, lean with a mild flavor, which makes them a blank canvas

for some of the many seasoning and marinade options.

- **Mackerel:** An oily fish with a bold flavor, it may not be the primary choice because it has more fat. However, its taste is robust and rich when you prepare it right.

- **Salmon:** Another oily fish, but salmon is a sturdy fish with a wonderful flavor. However, it doesn't have such a long shelf-life as other fish due to its fat content.

Other Choices

Venison:

The best cuts for deer jerky typically come from whole roasts cut from the deer's hind legs. This is because these cuts are easy to slice and hold together and are a little tougher than backstraps.

8. Venison is another option for making jerky. Source: FotoosVanRobin from Netherlands, CC BY-SA 2.0 <https://creativecommons.org/licenses/by-sa/2.0>, via Wikimedia Commons: https://commons.wikimedia.org/wiki/File:Venison_Steaks.jpg

Trim off as much fat as possible, and don't forget that meat shrinks in weight as it dries. If you slice a four-pound roast, you will get approximately a pound of dried jerky. You also need to ensure you cut off as much silver skin as you can. If you leave it on, this tough, sinewy muscle acts as dental floss!

Rabbit:

Virtually any cut from a rabbit can be used because it is one of the leanest meats around, with little to no fat.

Chicken and Turkey:

Use breast meat where possible, as it is the biggest cut and the leanest. It is also cheap compared to many other meats and is easy to cut.

Duck and Goose:

Again, use the breast meat, but bear in mind that both duck and goose are fatty. Remove as much fat as possible before you start slicing and drying it.

Important Tips:

No matter what cut you use for jerky, there are a couple of basic rules to follow:

- Never use meat that is past its best, as you won't get good jerky. It could even be unsafe to eat, no matter how well you heat and dry it.
- Don't forget that the quantity of jerky you get is about a third to a quarter of the original weight. Make sure you buy enough to get the quantity you want.
- Find the right cuts – don't just buy anything. Take your time, inspect the meat, and buy cuts with the least amount of fat.

Marinades and Seasonings

Marinating meat or fish requires submerging it in a liquid comprising oil, water, seasonings, cure, and acid. It is a vital part of the end product, determining texture, flavor, and shelf stability.

- **Flavor:** The flavor and aroma compounds soak into the meat or fish, imparting a unique flavor profile. Salt is the most critical component as it gets into more of the meat and seasons it all the way through.

- **Texture:** Using an acidic ingredient helps make the meat more tender as it helps break the muscle fibers down. You can use red, white, or balsamic vinegar, orange, lemon, or lime juice, or even pineapple.

- **Cure:** Cures need time to work and must have permanent contact with the meat. Most cures are made primarily from salt.

Marinades generally don't go any deeper than the meat's surface – the only thing that does is a cure. That means thin meat slices are best for jerky as more of the meat is seasoned and flavored.

Seasonings and Mixes:

9. *There are many ingredients you can use to season your jerky. Source: https://unsplash.com/photos/assorted-color-spoons-with-spices-V5Bqsot6UCg?utm_content=creditShareLink&utm_medium=referral&utm_source=unsplash*

Make sure you have what you need to make your jerky seasonings. These are some of the best and most popular ingredients:

- Black pepper
- Dried basil
- Dried rosemary
- Dried thyme
- Garlic powder
- Garlic salt
- Ground cumin
- Ground red pepper
- Hickory liquid smoke

- Lemon pepper seasoning
- McCormick Meat Marinade mix
- Onion salt
- Sea salt
- Seasoned salt
- Soy sauce
- Sugar
- Tabasco sauce
- Table salt
- Teriyaki sauce
- Traditional liquid smoke
- Vinegar
- Worcestershire sauce

Obviously, this is just the tip of the iceberg. There are tons more seasonings you can use, and the trick is to have as many to hand as possible to vary your recipes.

Choosing the Best Cuts

When you are buying meat to make jerky, there are certain things to remember:

1. Buy Lean Cuts

You'll read this advice several times – lean cuts make the best jerky. Fat content is critical when deciding on meat, as fat does not dehydrate properly. When you have too much fat in the meat, the resulting jerky may become rancid and go off quicker than jerky made from lean meat. However, if you intend to consume the jerky within a day or two, you can get away with a little more fat in the meat.

Not all fat is equal, though. You need to consider two types – intramuscular and intermuscular.

Intramuscular fat is the marbling seen in some cuts of meat. It is found between muscle fibers and can't be cut out. However, it does provide the meat with a lovely flavor and contributes to a tender, juicy finish, an important factor when you choose your meat.

In contrast, intermuscular is the fat found on the outside of lean meat, and this should be cut off before you make the jerky. Choose meat with the least amount of intermuscular fat for the best results. Although cuts with more marbling produce tender jerky, you should still choose cuts with little to no fat to ensure a longer shelf life.

2. Pick Economical Cuts

Quality is far more important than price, and the more expensive cuts are not always the best. In fact, you are better off not buying prime cuts. The sheer beauty in making jerky is that you can turn a tough cut into something tender and melt-in-the-mouth. Save the prime cuts for special meals, not making jerky.

3. Always Buy Fresh Meat

Never buy meat nearing or past its expiration date. The fresher the meat, the better and tastier your jerky will be, not to mention safer to eat. Inspect all meat before you buy it, and make sure it is the best it can be.

4. Buy Enough

Don't forget that a high percentage of the meat weight disappears when you dry it, so make sure you buy enough for what you want to make. The recommended ratio is 3:1. If you want a pound of jerky, buy three pounds of meat.

5. Get Friendly with Your Local Butcher

They are one of your best sources of meat, and you can even ask them to slice the meat for you, saving you a ton of time at home. Tell them how you want it, and they'll use their commercial slicer to produce exactly what you want. Cutting it evenly will ensure it dries evenly, a critical part of successful jerky.

6. Monitor the Sales

10. Keep an eye on sales and weekly specials. Source: https://unsplash.com/photos/yellow-sale-text-printed-on-glass-window-628M6D91QX0?utm_content=creditShareLink&utm_medium=referral&utm_source=unsplash

First, learn and understand the different cuts of meat, and then you can keep an eye on the sales and weekly specials. Head to big box stores to get great deals on large quantities– you can keep it in the freezer until you need it or spend the weekend making jerky.

Chapter 3: Jerky Preparation Techniques

Choosing your ingredients is just the first part of the process. More important is being able to turn those ingredients into something delicious. This chapter will teach the best ways to cut the meat, how to use ground meat to make jerky, and some of the best ways to dry it. You'll also learn why marinading meat before it is made into jerky is so important.

11. There are many ways to dry your jerky. Source: Stefano A. from Toronto, Canada, CC BY 2.0 <https://creativecommons.org/licenses/by/2.0>, via Wikimedia Commons: https://commons.wikimedia.org/wiki/File:Beef_jerky_being_dried.jpg

Slicing Your Meat to Perfection

Most people know how to carve a roast for dinner, but slicing meat for jerky is a little different. However, provided you follow a few simple tips, you'll have the perfect, consistent jerky with the chew you want.

Consistency is the name of the game, and all your strips need to be evenly sized so they all dry at the same time. This eliminates the issues of under or over-drying. The recommended size is 1/8 to ¼-inch thick.

You need to consider whether you want chewy or soft jerky. The former requires cutting with the grain, while the latter requires cutting against the grain.

The five tips below will help you learn how to slice your meat for the perfect jerky:

1. Chill the Meat

Fresh meat is incredibly pliable and not that easy to cut. First, wrap your meat (or fish) in plastic wrap and put it in the freezer until firm enough to slice but not frozen.

When you try to slice meat at room temperature, you will find it moves about too much and is hard to slice. Very cold meat is much easier, especially when you need even slices. How long you leave your meat in the freezer is down to the freezer and meat temperature. Check on it every half-hour, but be aware it can take an hour or more to get cold enough. While the meat is chilling, now's the time to get everything else you need together.

2. Trim the Fat

Before you even think about slicing the meat, you need to remove as much external fat as possible. When you work with natural ingredients, you get the beauty of there not being any uniformity. Every piece of meat will produce something different, and that's where the fun and the challenge lies.

How much external fat there is will depend entirely on what cut you are working with, as some have more fat than others. Take a venison loin, for example. This is far leaner and has far less external fat than a beef brisket flat with a thick fat layer. However, regardless of whether the meat is lean or fatty, you must cut off as much external fat as you can. You need to do this without cutting the meat so a little fat will be left on – that can't be helped. This will render during the process, so provided there is only a little, it won't make any real difference to the result. You can always remove the fat once it is cooked and dried.

Make sure you work with a sharp knife for this, as, strangely, dull knives can end in more accidents than sharp ones. That's because you will be forcing it into the fat. With a sharp knife, that doesn't happen. Always let the knife do the work for you, not the other way around.

3. Cut Large Pieces into Smaller Ones

Before you slice your meat into jerky strips, the next step is to cut large chunks of meat down into smaller ones. That makes them easier to manage, but it is dependent on the cut you are working with.

For example, if you choose a top round, you'll need to cut it down several times to get to the right size. If you choose an eye of round, on the other hand, you don't need to cut it down and can get right to cutting it into strips.

4. Choose Whether to Cut with or Against the Grain

This is your next decision, and it all comes down to whether you want traditional, chewy jerky or soft, tender jerky. First, you need to understand what the grain is. In meat, the grain indicates the direction of the muscle fibers, and you can find it by looking for steaks in your meat, usually accompanied by marbling, which is white.

If you want a traditional, chewy jerky, you need to slice along the grain, resulting in the muscle fibers retaining a little more moisture. You need to slice the meat along the grain for soft, tender jerky because it causes more moisture to come out of the muscle fibers.

Here's an overview:

CUT	MUSCLE FIBERS	SIZE	JERKY STYLE	MOISTURE
Against the Grain	This leaves shorter fibers, which breaks the meat down	Short but wide	Soft and tender, melt-n-the-mouth	Because moisture is lost through the fibers, the jerky isn't as moist.
With the grain	This leaves longer fibers, creating a tougher jerky	Thin but long	More like a traditional jerky, tougher and chewier	Has more moisture as the muscle fibers have not been cut through

5. Slice It into Strips

The final step is to cut your meat into the jerky strips. Use your non-dominant hand to secure the meat and slice it to the thickness you want, using even, long strokes and a sharp knife.

Getting each strip the same thickness is important, so try to get it between 1/8 and ¼-inch. Remember that the thicker the strips, the longer they take to process.

Practice really does make perfect here, but if you don't have the time to prepare, ask your butcher if they can do it for you. You'll get perfectly even slices, all ready to cook and dry.

Preparing Ground Meat

12. Ground meat can be used to make jerky. Source: Pannet, CC BY-SA 4.0 <https://creativecommons.org/licenses/by-sa/4.0>, via Wikimedia Commons: https://commons.wikimedia.org/wiki/File:%D0%A4%D0%B0%D1%80%D1%88.jpg

While traditional jerky is made from strips of whole meat, it is possible to make it from ground meat. This method allows you to make delicious jerky even on the slimmest of budgets because you can use cheaper cuts of meats. It isn't difficult, so long as you follow these steps:

1. Wash your cutting board and hands thoroughly.
2. Chop the meat into chunks small enough to fit your meat grinder.
3. Season the chunks all over to seal them in and grind them carefully, placing a clean container beneath the grinder to catch the ground meat.
4. Use your grinder's meat stomper to push the meat down into the throat so there is no waste.
5. Chill the ground meat for an hour or two in the refrigerator.
6. Meanwhile, clean the grinder. If you want even finer meat, run the ground meat through it again, then refrigerate again for a short while.
7. If you have already bought ready-ground meat, you can skip steps 2 onward and move straight to shaping the meat.

Shaping the Meat

1. Wash your hands thoroughly and wear disposable gloves for this.
2. Lay out a sheet of wax or freezer paper.
3. Mix your cure and seasoning into the meat, thoroughly combining and distributing it.
4. Spread the ground meat over the sheet of paper – if needed, use two or more sheets, depending on how much meat you are working with.

5. Place another sheet of paper over the top and roll the meat out so it is ¼-inch or less thick all over.
6. Peel the top sheet off and use a sharp, clean knife to slice the meat into inch-wide strips.
7. Lift the paper carefully onto a rack and flip it. Peel off the paper, leaving the strips of jerky on the rack.
8. Dry them using one of the methods below.

Traditional Drying Methods

Most people think that drying meat into jerky can only be done in an oven or dehydrator, but there are more ways to do it than that.

Below is an overview of five ways you can dry your jerky:

1. A Dehydrator

An electric dehydrator is undoubtedly one of the easiest ways to dry your meat, fish, or veggies into jerky. Your dehydrator must be set to 140°F, and the temperature must be maintained throughout the whole process. First, precook your meat strips until they have an internal temperature of 160°F (165°F for poultry.) Then, lay the strips on the drying racks, ensuring they do not touch or overlap – this reduces the risk of contamination and ensures the meat strips dry properly.

If you have a large dehydrator with two or more layers, switch the trays around every 30 to 60 minutes to ensure even dehydration. In the last 10 minutes of cooking, turn the heat down to just 10°F so your meat doesn't scorch.

2. Oven Drying

If a dehydrator is not an option, you can use your oven to dry your jerky. It doesn't need to be at a high temperature. In fact, lower temperatures work much better. You also don't need to use any setting other than baking.

13. You can use an oven to dry your jerky. Source: Myeyes.picture, CC BY-SA 4.0 <https://creativecommons.org/licenses/by-sa/4.0>, via Wikimedia Commons: https://commons.wikimedia.org/wiki/File:Oven_listrik.jpg

All ovens are different, and they all provide heat in different ways. To ensure your jerky dries properly, place a cookie sheet or a sheet of heavy-duty aluminum foil on the top shelf. This will help deflect the heat down. You should also leave the oven door open slightly to allow moisture to escape. You can use a wooden spoon to create the gap if you want. Lastly, stand a fan facing the oven and switch it on for air to circulate.

3. Sun Drying

This is one of the most traditional methods used for years to dry meat. However, it isn't considered efficient these days and won't work for many jerky types. Some that you can use sun drying for are:

- Lean beef

- Venison
- Young lamb

If you use this method, your strips of meat must be coated heavily in salt and left outside to dry in the sun. This only works if you live somewhere very hot but with decent breezes to help the air circulate and stop the meat from absorbing humid moisture from the atmosphere.

Typically, you don't preheat your meat strips to kill off the bacteria when you use the sun drying method, so there is some risk of bacteria. It's down to you to decide if the risk is worth the effort and time it will take. Do **NOT** use this method for poultry or fish, as these tend to be at a higher risk for pathogens and bacteria.

4. Smoker

The smoker is another traditional method of drying meat and is still popular today. However, you don't use the traditional drying teepees or rooms these days. Instead, you use modern smokers to keep a consistent 140°F temperature. It isn't a terribly convenient method, but if you've got all day and are prepared to keep the temperature consistent, go for it.

You can also only use certain woods for drying jerky, usually softwoods like pine, fir, or conifer. It gives your jerky a lovely smoky aroma and flavor, so it is worth the effort.

5. Microwave

The final method is using the microwave, but it isn't great. Microwaves do not provide even heat, and you won't get such good results as with other methods. That said, you can give it a go if you have no alternative.

Checking for Dryness

When you think the jerky is done, you need to check it. Lift a strip and leave it at room temperature to cool down, about five minutes should do it. Bend it at different sections. If it cracks, it is done. If not, dry it for a little while longer.

When your jerky is perfectly dry, lift it onto a rack coated in clean paper towels. This will absorb any grease from the meat as it cools down. Once it is cool, it can be packaged up and stored to keep it fresh for longer – you'll find out how to do that later in the book. The important thing is to keep it away from moisture and light.

In the early days, people didn't have refrigerators, so they soaked their meat in spices and salt and dried it to keep it fresh for longer. That's where jerky comes from, and it is perhaps more popular today than ever before.

Why Is Marination Important for Jerky?

Marinades are blends of different ingredients that improve the texture and taste of some foods, and they are used worldwide in all kinds of cooking. While marinades will work with many foods, they are best suited to meat or fish.

Many people confuse marinades and rubs, but they are completely different. While they both give the meat a wonderful flavor using spices, herbs, and salts, rubs do not include acids, such as citrus or vinegar, nor do they contain fruit enzymes. The most significant difference is that marinades are liquid, while rubs are dry. With a marinade, the food is soaked in the liquid for a set amount of time while rubs are rubbed into the meat.

How Marinades Work

When you marinate meat, you add flavor and a softer, tender texture. The enzymes or acid in the marinade break the meat surface down, allowing the liquid to soak into the meat.

Salt is a common marinade ingredient as it draws moisture from the meat. This moisture is then reabsorbed into the meat, along with the marinade ingredients, through osmosis. This allows the flavors to penetrate deep into the meat, and when you add oil to the mix, they carry the flavors of the spices, herbs, garlic, and whatever else you use deep into the meat, too.

So, there are two important reasons to marinate meat before turning it into jerky:

1. **Flavor:** How much flavor is added will depend entirely on what you use and how long you marinate the meat. Your options are endless, and while there will be some marinade recipes later in the book, you should let your creative side out and create your own delicious marinades.
2. **Texture:** Good marinades break the meat down, which means you can use cheaper, tougher cuts of meat for your jerky and still get a tender, soft result.

How to Marinate Beef Jerky

To give you an idea of how to marinate the meat, here's how to do beef jerky:

1. Get a Ziploc bag, lidded Tupperware container, or bowl with a lid – metal or glass only.

2. Put the beef strips in your chosen container. Make your marinade, pour it in, and mix it all around. Each beef strip must be coated in the marinade.

3. Remove as much oxygen as possible from the container or ensure the meat is completely submerged in the marinade so no air can get to it. Oxygen can cause the meat to discolor.

4. Refrigerate for as long as the recipe recommends, up to 24 hours unless specified. Stir the marinade a couple of times throughout the marination period to ensure the meat and marinade maintain contact.

The best container is a Ziploc bag, as it is easy to massage the marinade into the meat through the plastic without having to open it. However, once you have finished marinating the meat, dispose of the bag. Never reuse it for another batch, as this can lead to cross-contamination and the potential for bacteria.

Once you have marinated your meat, it's ready to be precooked and dried.

Chapter 4: Dehydrating and Smoking Jerky

Dehydrators and smokers are by far the best methods to dry your jerky. While an oven is a good option, it can take a long time, and you could end up with a bigger-than-expected power bill. Smokers and dehydrators are much cheaper and more efficient.

This chapter will go over how to use a dehydrator and a smoker to make the perfect jerky and finish with an overview of different jerky textures.

Making Jerky in a Dehydrator

14. Beef jerky can be made in a dehydrator. Source: Dennis Brown at English Wikipedia, CC BY-SA 3.0 <https://creativecommons.org/licenses/by-sa/3.0>, via Wikimedia Commons: https://commons.wikimedia.org/wiki/File:Raw_jerky_in_dehydrator.jpg

This section will focus on beef jerky, but you can use a dehydrator for any type, and the steps remain largely the same. The best way to show you how to use a dehydrator to make jerky is with a recipe, and this one includes two different flavors.

Teriyaki:

- **Brown Sugar:** perfect for sweetening and adding a caramelized taste. White sugar or sweetener will work, but brown is better.

- **Sesame Oil:** adds a nuttiness to the flavor, and only the tiniest bit is needed.

- **Rice Vinegar:** This provides acidity and a tangy aftertaste. It also provides balance for the other ingredients. You can also use regular white or apple cider vinegar if you don't have rice wine.

- **Ginger:** This adds a wonderful flavor that goes well with the other ingredients. Fresh ginger is best, but ground ginger will do as well. If you choose ground, you only need ½ a tsp, compared to an inch of fresh ginger.
- **Garlic:** This adds a beautiful, fresh flavor. Use fresh garlic if you can. A teaspoon of garlic powder will work if you can't get fresh.
- **Sesame Seeds:** Adds a lovely finishing look and a bit of crunch.
- **Pepper:** Adds a bit of a kick.

Smoky Pepper:

- **Liquid Smoke:** Provides a wonderful, deep flavor.
- **Worcestershire Sauce:** Adds a savory, salty flavor to the beef.
- **Onion Powder:** Add a light onion flavor.
- **Garlic Powder:** Freshens the taste and adds a nice kick.
- **Salt:** Balances the marinade and adds extra flavor.
- **Cracked Pepper:** Adds a bold kick with a peppery taste.

Tips on Using a Dehydrator

These are just a few tips for now to help when you get the full recipes later on.:

- **Use Lean Meat:** The leaner the meat, the better because you need as little fat as possible for this. Trim off any excess before you begin.

- **Cool the Meat:** Wrap the meat in plastic wrap and freeze it for a while, making it easier to slice.

- **Slice the Meat:** If your butcher won't slice the meat for you (most will if you ask them), you need a sharp knife. Slice the beef as thin as possible, no more than ¼-inch thick, and make sure it is no more than 2 inches wide and 4 inches long. Make sure you slice it against the grain if you want a tender jerky and with it if you want a chewier jerky.

- **Dry the Meat:** Use clean paper towels to pat the meat dry before you marinate it. This is important as you need the meat to dry out. Excess moisture in or on the meat will hamper this and slow down the process.

- **Marinate the Meat:** Make your marinade and soak the meat in it for as long as the recipe states – no more, no less. The easiest way is to put the marinade and beef in a Ziploc bag and mix it thoroughly. Lift it from the marinade and pat it dry again, ready for drying.

- **Dehydrate the Meat:** Lay the beef strips on the dehydrator trays, making sure they do not touch. There should be a little space to allow the air to circulate and dry the pieces evenly. Keep in mind that every dehydrator is different, and how long it takes will depend on the make and model. You should start checking on the meat at the 4-hour mark and then every half-hour. If some pieces dry quicker than others, remove them and spread the rest out.

- **Put It in the Oven:** This is optional, and you can do this before dehydrating it if you prefer. Lay the beef on a sheet pan and bake on the lowest heat for about 10 minutes.

Frequently Asked Questions

1. How Long Does Beef Jerky Take to Dry in a Dehydrator?

That depends on your model and how thick your beef slices are. They should be no more than ¼-inch thick and will take between four and six hours at 160°F to dry.

2. What Is the Best Cut?

Any lean cut of beef will work for beef jerky, so long as it is sliced thinly. Some of the best cuts are bottom round, top round, roulade, brisket, flank steak, and sirloin tip.

3. How Long Should It Be Marinated For?

This is a critical step to producing flavorful jerky, and, as a rule, the longer you can marinate the meat, the better the flavor and tenderer the meat. It should be marinated for at least four hours but no more than 24. Sticking it in the fridge overnight is best, but don't forget to stir the marinade around occasionally.

4. Is It Possible to Overcook the Beef in a Dehydrator?

Yes, it is. After four hours, you must start looking at the beef and then check it every 30 minutes. If any pieces are properly dry, remove them.

5. How Do You Know When the Jerky Is Ready?

Bend a piece. If it doesn't break but the top cracks, it is done. If not, carry on drying it. Dried jerky also looks dry and darker.

6. Does the Jerky Need to be Turned Over in the Dehydrator?

No, this is not necessary. Once you place the meat in the dehydrator, you don't need to do anything until it has been drying for four hours. The holes in the trays allow the air to circulate, drying the meat evenly. However, depending on your dehydrator, you may need to rotate the trays.

7. How Long Does Dehydrated Jerky Store?

It will last for up to two months at room temperature if it has been packaged and stored properly. You can store it in the fridge but it should be vacuum-packed. If it isn't, it can soak in moisture and that will mean a shorter time before it has to be eaten.

Teriyaki Beef:

Ingredients:

- 2 lb. of thinly sliced beef
- ½ cup of soy sauce
- ½ cup of brown sugar
- ¼ cup of rice wine vinegar
- 1 tbsp of sesame oil
- 1 tbsp of sesame seeds
- 4 minced garlic cloves
- 1-inch piece of minced ginger

- 1 tsp of ground black pepper

Instructions:

1. Use clean paper towels to get as much moisture off the beef as possible and put it in a bowl or a large re-sealable bag.

2. Whisk all the marinade ingredients until well combined, then pour them over the beef. Make sure all the beef is coated and massage it in. Seal the bag or container, put it in the fridge, and leave it for four to 24 hours.

3. Tip the beef into a colander and let the marinade drain off. Use clean paper towels to pat the excess off the beef and spread all the strips out on your dehydrator trays. Make sure to leave a bit of space between each one and use as many trays as needed.

4. Dry the beef for about four hours at 160°F and then see if it is dried enough. If not, dry for another half-hour and then check again. Continue doing this for 0 minutes at a time until it dries.

5. Turn your oven on to the lowest temperature setting and let it preheat.

6. Spread the beef jerky on a tray lined with aluminum foil, leaving space between each piece, and bake for 10 to 12 minutes.

7. Pat it dry and let it cool completely before storing it.

Smoky Pepper Beef

- 2 lb. of thinly sliced beef
- ½ cup of soy sauce

- 2 tbsp of Worcestershire sauce
- 2 tsp freshly cracked black pepper
- 1 tsp of liquid smoke
- 1 tsp of salt
- 1 tsp of onion powder
- ½ tsp of garlic powder

Instructions:

1. Use clean paper towels to get as much moisture off the beef as possible and put it in a bowl or a large resealable bag.
2. Whisk all the marinade ingredients until well combined, then pour them over the beef. Make sure all the beef is coated and massage it in. Seal the bag or container, put it in the fridge, and leave it for four to 24 hours.
3. Tip the beef into a colander and let the marinade drain off. Use clean paper towels to pat the excess off the beef and spread all the strips out on your dehydrator trays. Make sure to leave a bit of space between each one and use as many trays as needed.
4. Dry the beef for about four hours at 160°F and then see if it is dried enough. If not, dry for another half-hour and then check again. Continue doing this for 0 minutes at a time until it dries.
5. Turn your oven on to the lowest temperature setting and let it preheat.

6. Spread the beef jerky on a tray lined with aluminum foil, leaving space between each piece, and bake for 10 to 12 minutes.

7. Pat it dry and let it cool completely before storing it.

Making Jerky in a Smoker

If you own a smoker, you're in for a treat because there is so much you can do with one. Not only can you cook up huge joints of meat to tender, smoky perfection, but you can also make some wonderful snacks to keep you going, particularly jerky.

Jerky is packed with protein and is a delicious snack that packs a real punch. And using your smoker to make jerky is far easier than you might think. First, here are some tips for making the best jerky in a smoker:

1. Lean Meat Is Critical

As you already know, lean meat is key to good jerky. Fat won't dry properly, and you can't store it for as long as jerky is made from lean meat. Plus, fat can go rancid quickly, leaving you with a potentially harmful and bad-tasting product.

Jerky is normally made from beef, but you can use many other cuts of meat, including game meats, poultry, lamb, pork, and fish and vegetables.

2. Slice Against the Grain

Again, you already know this. Slicing against the grain gives you perfect, tender jerky you can bite through without it being too tough. Jerky should never be so tough that you need to tug at it to get it to break.

3. Thin, Even Cuts

This is especially true with making jerky in a smoker. If the pieces are not all evenly sliced, some will dry quicker than others, and you could end up with burnt or undercooked strips. Don't forget to remove the fat too.

4. Season the Meat

While marination or seasoning is not a requirement, it makes for much better jerky, especially when smoked. Soak the meat strips in your choice of marinade and refrigerate for several hours. Here's a great recipe for beef jerky marinade:

- ½ cup of soy sauce
- 2 tbsp of honey
- 2 tbsp of Worcestershire sauce
- 1 tbsp of crushed red pepper flakes
- 2 tsp of garlic powder
- 2 tsp of onion powder
- 1 tsp of black pepper

Whisk it all together and soak the beef in it.

5. Drain the Marinade

When you make jerky, you want the meat dried out, so when you lift the meat from the marinade, you must let any excess drip off and then drain the strips on paper towels to remove the rest. Once done, the strips are ready to go in the smoker.

6. Hang Them

If there is enough room between the grates and the base of the smoker (a vertical smoker is ideal), you can hang the meat to dry. While you can lay them on the grates, hanging them helps them dry more evenly, and, often, it's a quicker method.

Simply slide a toothpick through the end of a strip or slide several strips onto a long skewer evenly spaced. Then, rest the toothpick or skewer on the grate while the strips hang down. Do soak the skewers or toothpicks in water for several minutes first. That way, they won't catch fire.

7. No Overlapping

You must not overlap any of the strips, or they will not dry out properly. If your smoker isn't big enough, you'll need to dry your meat in batches or use another method.

8. When to Use Liquid in the Smoker's Water Pan

If your meat has been soaked in a liquid marinade, there is no need to add water to the water pan. That would just add even more moisture to the meat's surface, and that's not what you want. However, if you use a dry rub instead, you can add some liquid to the pan, but only for the first one to two hours of smoking time.

9. Don't Use Strong Wood

The wood you use in the smoker will impart a flavor to the meat, so be wary of using wood with a strong flavor, such as Mesquite. Instead, use milder woods like pecan, oak, apple, or hickory.

10. Keep the Temperature Low and Consistent

Don't forget, you are not cooking a joint of meat. To get your jerky nice and dry, it needs to be smoked at a consistently low temperature between 150 and 170°F. You could go to 200° at a push, but any higher, and you run the risk of burning the meat.

11. The Smoke Should be Blue and Thin

If you have your smoker at the correct temperature, the smoke will be a thin, blue stream. If it is billowing out in white clouds, open the vents and slightly increase the temperature. White smoke gives the jerky a bitter taste.

12. Know How Long to Smoke It For

There is no one answer to this, as all smokers differ. It will take at least three hours and could be up to ten, depending on how thick the meat is and on your smoker model. For example, a pellet smoker at 200°F will take approximately three to five hours, while an electric smoker could take six to eight hours.

Start checking at three hours, then every hour after until the jerky is done. If any slices dry quicker, remove them so they don't burn. To check the jerky, take a slice out and leave it to cool down for up to 10 minutes. Then, bend it. The jerky is done if it is bendy and the surface cracks but doesn't break. If you see small white fibers inside, this also indicates the meat is done.

Different Jerky Textures

Some people love the smoky taste of some jerky. Others love all the different flavors, while some like the fact that it is a portable, clean snack to carry around. However, one thing that most jerky aficionados comment on is texture.

Enthusiasts expect a certain texture when they eat jerky, and if it's poor, it can really ruin your experience. Homemade jerky should have one of three textures, and we'll talk about those later.

First, why is texture an important factor in jerky? Here's why.

Why Is Texture So Important

15. Texture is an important factor when it comes to jerky. Source: Larry Jacobsen from Cheyenne Wyoming, CC BY 2.0 <https://creativecommons.org/licenses/by/2.0>, via Wikimedia Commons: https://commons.wikimedia.org/wiki/File:Jerky_(1).jpg

So, what's the fuss over jerky texture? If you only ever buy jerky from the stores, you'll be used to the texture of commercial, mass-produced jerky. That might be good enough for you, but homemade jerky has so much more going for it.

The history of jerky you read earlier in the book is important in terms of texture because it indicates the evolvement of this iconic snack from a much-needed food source to a snack people enjoy today because they want to. Over time, textures have changed due to different drying processes, but you really want to be aiming for one of three textures – or a combination of all three.

- **Old-Fashioned:** Typically called "cowboy jerky," this has a salty, tough texture and is usually created by smoking. Tough, chewy jerky takes longer to eat, so you won't need so much to satisfy your hunger. And, because you are chewing more, your mouth produces more saliva, and this brings the flavor in the jerky out.

- **Traditional:** You are likely used to this texture as it's the one produced by big-brand jerky manufacturers. Although it follows the same preparation as old-fashioned, it is marinaded in an acidic, sugary liquid for longer, making it softer than old-fashioned jerky. This is considered a great texture as it gives the satisfaction of a chewy jerky without being too dry.

- **Soft and Tender:** In the early days, jerky was considered a whole food, and it was typically made from beef and game animals. However, more recently, things have begun to change, and manufacturers have started to produce gourmet versions. People who loved the classic jerky were not happy with this but the market was suddenly blown wide open, attracting people who hadn't liked traditional jerky. Some gourmet jerkies differed from the traditional by being tender and soft, made with a range of ingredients and seasonings that helped break down the tough muscle fibers and make the meat softer. Jerky made from poultry is typically softer than meat, but beef and other meat cuts can also be tender and soft with the right preparation.

There is no "best" option because that is a personal choice. What is important is how you choose to make yours and make sure you follow the right method to get what you want.

Chapter 5: Jerky Recipes for Different Proteins

Now for the fun part – the recipes. This chapter is quite long, but you will find plenty of recipes covering beef, chicken, turkey, game, and a whole section dedicated to vegan and vegetarian jerky. Don't forget that these recipes are just ideas. Once you are confident making your own jerky, get creative and play around with the recipes to create unique variations. Note there are various methods here – oven, dehydrator, and smoker, but don't be afraid to experiment with each recipe and see what methods work best for you. You can also make these recipes just using the dry ingredients. When you take liquid out of the equation, you've got the makings of a tasty dry rub.

16. There are many recipes for making jerky. Source: Pannet, CC BY-SA 4.0 <https://creativecommons.org/licenses/by-sa/4.0>, via Wikimedia Commons: https://commons.wikimedia.org/wiki/File:%D0%94%D0%B6%D0%B5%D1%80%D0%BA%D0%B8.jpg

Beef

Beef Jerky

Ingredients:

- 3 lb. piece of eye of round, fat, and silver skin trimmed off
- 1 packed cup of dark brown sugar
- 1 cup of soy sauce
- 3 tbsp of Worcestershire sauce
- 1 tbsp of smoked paprika
- 1 tsp of onion powder
- 1 tsp of freshly ground black pepper

- 1 tsp of crushed red pepper flakes
- 1 tsp of meat tenderizer – unseasoned
- 1 tsp of smoked paprika
- ½ tsp of garlic powder

Instructions:

1. Once you have trimmed the meat, slice it with the grain into pieces 1/8 to ¼-inch thick. If it is too big to handle, slice the roast in half first.
2. Make the marinade. Put all the remaining ingredients in a bowl, give it a good stir, and make sure the sugar has dissolved completely.
3. Put the meat in the bowl with the marinade. Toss it to make sure the meat is coated and put a lid or clean towel over the bowl. Alternatively, transfer the meat and marinade into a large Ziploc bag, seal it, and massage the contents.
4. Refrigerate for at least 12 hours, stirring it or tossing the bag a couple of times to keep the meat coated.
5. Preheat your oven to 175°F, set two racks in the center, and place aluminum foil over two baking sheets. Put one beneath each rack to catch the drips.
6. Remove the beef from the marinade, pat the excess off, and lay the strips on the racks in one layer. Bake for 3 to 4 hours, rotating the racks from top to bottom and turning them around halfway through to ensure the meat dries evenly.
7. Remove one piece, let it cool, then bend it. It is done if it doesn't break but looks leathery and is chewy but tender.

8. Set the jerky somewhere to cool down completely, then put it in a resealable bag or airtight container. You can store this somewhere dark and cool until ready to eat.

Garlic Black Pepper Beef Jerky

Ingredients:

- 1 lb. of lean eye of round roast
- ¼ cup of soy sauce
- ¼ cup of cold water
- 2 tbsp of brown sugar
- 2 tsp of ground black pepper
- ½ tsp of garlic powder
- ½ tsp of sea salt
- ¼ tsp of onion powder
- ¼ tsp of curing salt – Prague Powder #1 – OPTIONAL

Instructions:

1. Cut as much visible fat off the meat as possible, wrap it up in plastic wrap or baking paper, and freeze it. Don't leave it for more than two hours.
2. While the meat is freezing, whisk the marinade ingredients together in a large bowl or resealable bag and set it aside.
3. Take the meat out and slice it against the grain into ¼-inch thick slices if you want a tender jerky, with the grain if you want it chewy.

4. Place the beef slices in the marinade, massage it in, and seal the bag or container. Refrigerate for eight to 24 hours.

5. Remove the beef from the marinade and shake off the excess. Pat it dry with clean paper towels.

Decide whether to use your oven, smoker, or dehydrator to dry the beef strips.

- **Oven:** Preheat the oven to 170°F to 200°F. Place a sheet of aluminum foil over the bottom rack and layer the beef on the top rack, or use soaked toothpicks or a skewer to suspend them from the rack. Prop the door open a little and dry them for three to eight hours. Check at the three-hour mark and then every half hour or so until they are done.

- **Smoker:** Preheat the smoker to 170°F and place aluminum foil over the drip pan. Suspend the strips from the top rack using a soaked toothpick or a skewer and smoke for 1 ½ hours with the top vent open. Raise the temperature to 180°F to 200°F, add soaked wood chips, and continue smoking for up to an hour or until the smoke turns blue. Turn the temperature back down to 160°F, open the wood tray door halfway, and continue smoking until done. This is for an electric smoker; follow the manufacturer's instructions if you have a pellet smoker.

- **Dehydrator:** Set the dehydrator to 160°F, layer the beef strips evenly over the trays, and follow the manufacturer's instructions to dry the beef. After three hours, check the meat. Take out any pieces that are done and let the rest cook in half-hour increments until it is all done.

Ground Beef Jerky

Ingredients:

- 1 lb. of lean ground beef
- 2 tbsp of Worcestershire sauce
- 2 tbsp of soy sauce
- 1 tsp of lemon pepper
- 1 tsp of ground black pepper
- 1 tsp of red curry powder
- 1 tsp of onion powder
- 1 tsp of garlic powder
- 1 tsp of ginger powder
- 2 tsp of liquid smoke – OPTIONAL
- ¼ tsp of curing salt - OPTIONAL

Instructions:

1. Put all the ingredients in a big non-reactive bowl.
2. Use a wooden spoon or clean hands to combine everything thoroughly – you can premix the marinade ingredients to ensure they are evenly distributed.
3. Place a sheet of baking paper on a flatboard and cover it with wax paper. Lay the ground beef on the paper, cover it with another sheet of wax paper, and roll it to an even ¼-inch thick all over.
4. Slice it into strips an inch thick and four to five inches long.

5. Choose how you want to dry them. A dehydrator works best for ground beef, so set it at 160°F and dry it for three hours before checking. Continue in half-hour increments until the beef is dried.

Smoked Beer Jerky

Ingredients:

- 1 lb. of lean eye of round
- ¼ cup of soy sauce
- ¼ cup of Worcestershire sauce
- ¼ cup of dark or smoked beer
- 1 tbsp of freshly cracked black pepper
- 1 tsp of onion powder
- 1 tsp of honey
- ¼ tsp of curing salt #1 – OPTIONAL

Instructions:

1. Cut off the visible fat and freeze it for about an hour, wrapped in plastic or baking paper.
2. Whisk the marinade ingredients in a big bowl or resealable bag.
3. Slice the meat 1/8 to ¼-inch thick – with or against the grain, however you want your jerky.
4. Place the meat in the marinade, make sure it is fully covered, then refrigerate for six to 24 hours – the longer, the better.

5. Tip the beef into a colander and drain off the marinade. Pat the excess off with clean paper towels and dry it with the method you prefer.

Spicy Sweet Beef Jerky

Ingredients:

- 1 lb. of top round
- ¼ cup of soy sauce
- ¼ cup of cold water
- 2 tbsp of dark brown sugar
- 1 tbsp of lemon juice
- 1 tbsp of honey
- 2 tsp of rice wine vinegar
- 2 tsp of crushed red pepper flakes
- 1 tsp of Dijon mustard
- 1 tsp of freshly cracked black pepper
- 1 tsp of ground ginger
- ½ tsp of garlic powder
- ¼ tsp of sesame oil

Instructions:

1. Cut off the visible fat and let the meat cool in the freezer for up to two hours.
2. Put all the marinade ingredients in a resealable bag or big non-reactive bowl.

3. Take the meat from the freezer and cut it along or across the grain – depends how you like your jerky – into ¼-inch strips.
4. Marinate the beef for six to 24 hours before straining the marinade and patting off the excess.
5. Dry it using your chosen method.

Tequila Beef Jerky

Ingredients:

- 1 lb. of top round roast
- ¼ cup of cold water
- 2 tbsp of Tequila
- 1 tbsp of freshly squeezed lime juice
- 1 tsp of freshly cracked black pepper
- ½ tsp of garlic powder
- ½ tsp of cayenne pepper
- ½ tsp of kosher salt
- ½ tsp of onion powder
- ¼ tsp of curing salt #1 – OPTIONAL

Instructions:

1. Trim the meat and partially freeze it to firm it up.
2. Make the marinade by combining the liquid ingredients and then whisking in the dry ingredients. Add to a Ziploc bag or container.
3. Slice the meat into ¼-inch strips – with the grain for a chewy jerky, against it for a softer jerky.

4. Place the meat in the marinade and refrigerate for eight to 24 hours.
5. Drain the marinade, pat the excess off using clean paper towels, and dry it using your favorite method.

Brisket Beef Jerky

Ingredients:

- 1 lb. of lean beef – your choice of cut
- 1 cup of Allegro brisket sauce
- 2 tsp of hickory liquid smoke
- ¼ tsp of curing salt # 1 – OPTIONAL

Instructions:

1. Cut off the fat and put the meat in the freezer for a couple of hours.
2. Mix the marinade ingredients in a resealable bag or big bowl.
3. Slice the meat into ¼-inch thick strips with or against the grain, depending on how you want your jerky.
4. Marinate the beef in the mixture for eight to 24 hours, then drain it and pat off the excess marinade.
5. Dry it using your smoker, oven, or dehydrator.

BBQ Beef Jerky

Ingredients:

- 1 ½ lb. of flank steak
- ½ cup of ketchup
- ¼ cup of brown sugar

- 1/3 cup of red wine vinegar
- 2 tbsp of curing salt
- 2 tbsp of hickory liquid smoke
- 1 tbsp of dry mustard
- 1 tbsp of onion powder
- ½ tsp of garlic powder
- ¼ tsp of cayenne pepper

Instructions:

1. Cut the fat off and let the beef freeze a little, no more than two hours – you don't want it frozen solid.
2. Cut it no more than 1/8th-inch thick against the grain.
3. Add the red wine vinegar and sugar to a small pan and heat it over low heat to dissolve the sugar.
4. Add the ketchup, salt, liquid smoke, mustard powder, onion powder, garlic powder, and cayenne pepper and stir, heating until you have a smooth consistency. Set it aside to cool.
5. Put the beef strips in a large bowl or resealable bag, add the beef strips, and mix it all up. Make sure the beef is coated all over, cover the bowl, and put it in the fridge for eight hours or more – the longer the better.
6. Set your oven to preheat to 190°F to 230°F – whichever is lowest on your oven. Place foil over the racks and place the beef strips in one layer, not overlapping.
7. Leave the door propped open a little and cook for three to four hours or until dry. Check after three hours and continue until dried.

8. Use clean paper towels to remove the excess grease and leave the strips to cool down.

Bourbon Beef Jerky

Ingredients:
- 3 lb. of topside beef
- 2 cups of ketchup
- 1 cup of Bourbon
- ½ cup of brown sugar
- ¼ cup of balsamic vinegar
- 2 tbsp of Worcestershire sauce
- 2 tbsp of liquid smoke
- 2 tbsp of wholegrain mustard
- 3 minced garlic cloves
- 1 tbsp of chipotle chili powder
- 1 tbsp of ancho chili powder
- 1 tbsp of molasses

Instructions:
1. Cut the fat off and cool the beef until frozen enough to slice but not frozen solid.
2. Cut it into strips about 1/8th inch wide.
3. Mix the marinade ingredients in a saucepan. Stir it frequently while heating it over low heat.
4. Allow it to cool down before pouring it over the beef in a Ziploc bag or large container. Marinate for at least eight hours.

5. Preheat your oven to its lowest heat setting and line the racks with aluminum foil.
6. Lay the beef strips on the racks, leave the oven door propped open a little, and cook until dry – check after three hours.
7. Pat off the excess fat and set the jerky aside. Once it has cooled down completely, you can store it.

Mexican Lime Beef Jerky

Ingredients:

- 2 lb. of top round
- 1 cup of Mexican beer
- 2 medium jalapeno peppers
- ½ a medium red onion
- ½ cup of freshly squeezed lime juice
- 1 tbsp of fresh mint leaves
- 1 tsp of Mexican oregano

Instructions:

1. Trim the fat and freeze the beef for an hour until firm enough to slice easily.
2. Slice it along the grain into 1/8-inch thick strips.
3. Finely chop the pepper and onion. Add them to a blender with the oregano and mint, and blend it on high – you want a smooth paste, no chunks.
4. Pour the lime juice and beer into the blender and blitz to combine it. Pour the marinade into a resealable bag or big bowl and add the beef. Mix to coat the beef and

leave it at room temperature for about four to six hours.

5. Preheat your oven to its lowest heat setting and line the racks with aluminum foil.

6. Layer the beef strips in a single layer and leave the oven door open a little.

7. Cook for about three hours, then check it. Continue cooking for half an hour at a time until completely dry,

8. Use clean paper towels to remove the grease from the jerky. Set the meat aside and let it cool right down before you store it.

Poultry

BBQ Chicken Jerky

Ingredients:

- 2 ½ lb. of skinless, boneless chicken breast
- ½ cup of BBQ sauce
- 2 tbsp of Worcestershire sauce
- 1 tbsp of salt
- 1 tbsp of brown sugar
- 1 tbsp of minced garlic
- 1 tbsp of hickory liquid smoke
- 1 tbsp of onion powder

Instructions:

1. Put the chicken in the freezer for an hour to make it easier to slice. Cut it into long strips about ¼-inch wide.
2. Put the salt, sugar, and liquid smoke in a small bowl, mix it thoroughly, and coat the chicken strips all over. Put them in the fridge for one hour.
3. While the jerky is in the fridge, make another marinade using the remaining ingredients.
4. Get the jerky strips out of the fridge, use clean paper to dry them gently, and drop them in the other marinade. Leave them in the fridge overnight.
5. Turn your oven on and preheat it on the lowest heat setting. Wrap the racks in foil.
6. Layer the chicken strips on the racks, leave the oven door open a bit, and cook for three hours before checking them. These will take up to four hours to dry.
7. Let the jerky dry off somewhere cool and dry overnight before storing.

Drunken Chicken Jerky

Ingredients:

- 1 lb. of lean chicken breast
- ½ cup of red wine
- ¼ cup of Tequila
- ¼ cup of beer
- ¼ packed cup of brown sugar
- ¼ cup of teriyaki sauce

- ¼ cup of soy sauce
- 1 tbsp of liquid smoke
- 1 tsp of Tabasco sauce

Instructions:

1. Cut the fat off, wrap the chicken in plastic wrap, and freeze it – no more than an hour or two, just enough to firm it up.
2. Cut the chicken into long strips, about 1/8th inch thick.
3. Put the remaining ingredients in a resealable bag or non-reactive bowl, mix them all together, and add a little salt and pepper to taste.
4. Put the chicken strips in the marinade and make sure every strip is coated all over. Leave it at room temperature for several hours – overnight is best.
5. Pour the chicken into a colander and let the marinade drain off. Pat each strip with clean paper towels to remove the excess.
6. Set your oven to its lowest heat setting and wrap foil over the racks.
7. Lay the chicken strips on the racks and bake with the oven door propped open for about three hours or until fully dry.
8. Allow them to cool off overnight somewhere cool and dry before storing them.

Ingredients:

- 3 lb. of boneless, skinless chicken breast
- ¾ cup of soy sauce

- ¾ cup of teriyaki sauce
- ½ cup of honey
- 2 tbsp of rock salt
- 1 tbsp of sesame oil
- 1 tsp of garlic powder
- 1 tsp of onion powder

Instructions:

1. Trim the fat from the chicken and freeze it for an hour, no more than two.
2. Cut the chicken into long strips, about 1/8th inch thick.
3. Mix the salt and sesame oil together and rub each strip with it, massaging it all over.
4. Mix the rest of the ingredients together in a bowl or resealable bag and add the chicken strips. Stir to make sure every strip is coated and refrigerate for several hours.
5. Preheat the oven to 180°F and 220°F and line the racks with aluminum foil.
6. Lay the chicken strips on the racks and bake for three hours before checking them. Continue checking every half hour until they are done. Don't forget to leave the door open a little to allow the air to circulate.
7. Remove the grease using clean paper towels and set them aside to cool off – leave them overnight.

The jerky will keep for around three months if you store it in a dry, airtight container.

Buffalo Chicken Jerky

Ingredients:

- 1 lb. of lean ground chicken
- ¼ cup of hot sauce
- 2 tbsp of Worcestershire sauce
- 2 tbsp of Tabasco sauce
- 1 tsp of garlic powder
- 1 tsp of salt
- 1 tsp of onion powder
- ½ tsp of ground celery seeds
- ½ tsp of ground black pepper

Instructions:

1. Put the chicken in a large bowl.
2. Mix the rest of the ingredients (not the Tabasco or Worcestershire sauces) and pour it all into the bowl with chicken. Combine using a wooden spoon or clean hands, then refrigerate overnight.
3. Place a sheet of wax paper on a flat baking tray and put the meat on it. Add another sheet of paper and roll it flat until it is 1/8 to ¼-inch thick and even. Freeze for about half an hour.
4. Set your oven to 190°F and cover the racks with a sheet of foil.
5. Cut the meat thinly. Mix the Tabasco and Worcestershire sauces and coat each chicken strip with it.

6. Lay the strips on a rack and bake for 6 hours with the door open a little.
7. Once the jerky is done, raise the heat to 300°F and bake for 15 minutes.
8. Allow it to cool right down overnight in a cool, dry place, and then store it.

Ginger Lime Chicken Jerky

Ingredients:

- 2 lb. of lean chicken breast
- ½ cup of soy sauce
- ¼ cup of lime juice
- 2 tbsp of palm sugar
- 2 tbsp of minced fresh ginger
- 1 tbsp of minced fresh garlic
- 1 tbsp of diced fresh cilantro leaves
- 1 tsp of ground black pepper
- ½ tsp of salt

Instructions:

1. Take as much visible fat off as you can and wrap the chicken in plastic wrap. Cool it in the freeze for about an hour.
2. Cut the chicken into strips, about 1/8th inch thick.
3. Mix the sugar and lime juice in a small saucepan. Stir it constantly while heating it over low heat, to make sure the sugar dissolves completely. Take the pan off

the heat, add the rest of the ingredients, and stir it – this is the marinade.

4. Put the chicken and marinade in a resealable bag or bowl and mix together. Leave it at room temperature for at least eight hours, no more than 12. Then, lift the chicken out and pat it dry.

5. Set your oven to 190°F and lay aluminum foil over the base – this will catch the marinade drips, saving you from having to scrub your oven clean.

6. Put the strips of chicken onto clean, soaked, wooden skewers, leaving a gap between each piece. Place the skewers over the grill racks so the chicken hangs down.

7. Prop your oven door open just a bit, and let the chicken dry until it is chewy and tender – about three or four hours.

8. Set the chicken aside somewhere to cool overnight and then you can put it in an airtight container or vacuum-seal it for long-term storage.

Smoky Chicken Jerky

Ingredients:

- 1 ½ lb. of boneless, skinless chicken breast
- ¾ cup of soy sauce
- ¼ cup of teriyaki sauce
- 1 tbsp of Worcestershire sauce
- 2 tsp of dried parsley
- 1 tsp of smoked salt

- 1 tsp of lemon juice
- 1 tsp of garlic powder
- 1 tsp of ground ginger
- 1 tsp of ground black pepper
- 1 tsp of cayenne – OPTIONAL
- Cooking spray

Instructions:

1. Partly freeze the chicken, making it easier to slice. Then, cut it into strips about ¼-inch thick.
2. Put the marinade ingredients in a resealable bag and mix them up. Add the chicken and massage it to make sure every strip is coated. Seal the bag, making sure to remove the excess air.
3. Place the bag in the refrigerator and leave it overnight.
4. Set your oven to 180°F and coat the cooking rack with spray oil. Line a baking tray with foil and put the coated rack on top of it.
5. Drain the chicken and pat off the excess marinade. Lay them evenly on the rack and bake for four to five hours. Turn them halfway through cooking. They are done when they are dried and orange.

Turmeric Thyme Chicken Jerky

Ingredients:

- 2 to 3 whole chicken breasts, no skin or bones
- 1 cup of water + extra
- 1 tbsp of honey

- 1 tsp of turmeric
- 1 tsp of chopped fresh thyme
- ½ tsp of ground ginger

Instructions:

1. Cut the fat off the chicken and put it in the freezer for an hour or two. When they are firm, cut them into strips about ¼-inch thick.
2. Put the turmeric, ginger, honey, and water in a bowl, mix it well, and transfer it to a sealable bag.
3. Put the chicken in, adding more water to ensure the meat is covered. Massage it and refrigerate for about an hour.
4. Set your oven to 180°F and place a sheet of foil on a baking tray.
5. Tip the chicken into a colander and drain off the marinade, patting off the excess with clean paper towels. Put the strips in a single layer on the lined sheet, leaving ½-inch between them. Sprinkle the chopped thyme over the top.
6. Dry the chicken for three or four hours, leaving the oven door propped open just a little.
7. Set the strips to one side and let them cool off completely overnight.

Air Fryer Chicken Jerky

Ingredients:

- 1 lb. of lean chicken breast
- 1 cup of soy sauce

- 2 tbsp of ground ginger
- 2 tbsp of brown sugar or honey
- 2 tbsp of Chinese five-spice powder
- 1 tbsp of garlic powder
- ½ tsp of crushed red pepper flakes
- ¼ tsp of ground black pepper

Instructions:

1. Cool the chicken in the freezer until it is firm enough to slice but not frozen solid. Slice it into strips about 1/8th to ¼-inch thick. Soak wooden skewers in cold water.
2. Put all the other ingredients in a resealable bag and mix them up. Add the chicken, massage to coat, and marinate for 60 minutes or more.
3. Preheat the air fryer to 180°F for ten minutes and cut the bamboo skewers to fit the basket.
4. Drain the marinade, remove any excess, and thread the strips onto the skewers, leaving a little room between them.
5. Thread them into the basket and cook for 1 hour and 15 minutes – check on it after an hour. Turn the temperature up to 200°F and bake for 15 minutes.
6. Remove the chicken and place it somewhere cool and dry to cool off overnight.

Air Fryer Jalapeno Garlic Chicken Jerky

Ingredients:

- 3 medium-sized chicken breasts

- 1 finely chopped yellow onion
- 1 diced head of garlic
- 3 to 4 thinly sliced jalapenos
- 2 chopped bunches of fresh cilantro
- 2 tsp of white wine vinegar
- 1 ½ tsp of salt
- 1 tsp of onion powder
- 1 tsp of garlic powder
- ¼ tsp of ground black pepper

Instructions:

1. Firm the chicken up for an hour or so in the freezer before slicing it into strips about ¼ to 3/8th-inch thick.
2. Stir the jalapenos, salt, onions, pepper, and garlic in a large bowl.
3. Stir in the vinegar, garlic powder, onion powder, pepper, and salt, and transfer the mixture to a resealable bag.
4. Put the chicken strips in the bag, remove the air, and seal the bag before shaking it to mix everything together. Refrigerate for at least four hours, no more than 10.
5. Put some bamboo skewers into cold water and let them soak for 10 to 15 minutes – this will stop them from burning.
6. Pour the chicken into a colander to drain off the marinade.

7. Place the strips onto the skewers, leaving a bit of space between them.

8. Spray olive oil over the air fryer cooking basket and fix the skewers at the top, allowing the chicken to hang down.

9. Spray olive oil over the tops and air fry for 2 hours at 170°F. Then, turn the temperature up to 280°F and cook for 10 minutes until the internal temperature is 165°F.

10. Take the chicken out of the oven and lay the strips on a rack. Set them aside and store them when fully cool.

Turkey Jerky

Ingredients:

- 1 lb. of skinless, boneless turkey breast
- ¼ cup of Worcestershire sauce
- ¼ cup of soy sauce
- 1 tbsp of brown sugar
- 1 tbsp of hickory liquid smoke - OPTIONAL
- 1 tsp of onion powder
- 1 tsp of garlic powder
- ¼ tsp of curing salt – OPTIONAL

Instructions:

1. Put the turkey in the freezer for an hour or so until firm enough to slice. Cut off as much fat as possible and slice the meat into strips about ¼-inch thick.

2. Mix everything else in a bowl or bag and put the meat strips in. Massage so all the strips are coated and put in the fridge for at least 12 hours, up to 24.

3. Drain the turkey in a colander and discard the marinade. Pat clean kitchen towels over the meat to remove the excess.

4. Lay the strips in single layers on the dehydrator trays with a gap between each one.

5. Set the dehydrator to 160°F and dry the turkey for up to six hours. Start checking it at three hours and keep checking every half hour until it is all dried.

6. Alternatively, smoke them in a smoker for an hour, then transfer them to the dehydrator to get the right texture with a wonderful smoky flavor.

Ground Turkey Jerky

Ingredients:

- 1 lb. of dark and white ground turkey meat
- 1 tbsp of coconut aminos
- 1 tbsp of maple syrup or honey
- Juice and zest from a whole lemon
- 1 tbsp of onion powder
- 1 tsp of garlic granules
- 1 tsp of sea salt
- 1 tsp of ground black pepper

Instructions:

1. Mix all the marinade ingredients in a bowl. Add the turkey, wash your hands, and mix it all together. Set it aside for a couple of hours.

2. Place a sheet of parchment paper about the size of a dehydrator tray on a flat surface. Divide the meat mixture in two and place half on the paper. Place another sheet over the top and roll the meat until it is about ¼-inch thick. Take the top paper off, and slice the turkey into strips about 1 ½ inches wide. Arrange them on the dehydrator trays and do the same with the rest of the meat mixture.

3. Dry the meat in the dehydrator at 155°F for four to six hours or until dried to your liking. You don't want them brittle as they will dry further. Check the meat occasionally and pat off any excess oil, as this can make the jerky go rancid.

4. Preheat your oven to 275°F. Once it has reached temperature, lift the jerky onto a baking sheet and bake for 10 minutes. Take the jerky from the oven and put it on a plate. Set it aside to cool right down before you store it.

Variations:

You can vary this recipe by adding these ingredients to the marinade:

Rosemary and Thyme:

- 1 tbsp of finely chopped fresh rosemary OR 1/3 tbsp of dried
- 1 tbsp of finely chopped fresh thyme OR 1/3 tbsp of dried

Maple Sage:

- 1 tbsp of dark maple syrup
- 2 tbsp of finely chopped fresh sage OR 2/3 tbsp of dried

Basil Rosemary:

- 2 tbsp of finely chopped fresh basil OR 2/3 tbsp of dried
- 1 tbsp of finely chopped fresh rosemary OR 1/3 tbsp of dried

Spicy Turkey Jerky

Ingredients:

- 2 lb. of skinless, boneless turkey breast
- ½ cup of soy sauce
- 2 tbsp of honey
- 1 tbsp of garlic paste
- 1 tbsp of chili paste
- 2 tsp of dried red chili flakes

Instructions:

1. Cut off the fat and put it in the freezer for no more than two hours.
2. Cut the turkey into strips about 1/8th-inch thick.
3. Put everything else in a bowl and make your marinade, seasoning to taste with salt and pepper.

4. Put the turkey strips in the marinade and leave it at room temperature for several hours, preferably overnight.

5. Set your oven to its lowest setting and place foil over a couple of baking trays.

6. Drain the turkey, removing any excess marinade with clean paper towels.

7. Place the turkey strips on the trays, keeping them a little way apart, and bake for three hours or until flexible and dry. Make sure the door is left open a little to let moisture out of the oven.

8. When the jerky is dry, let it cool down overnight and then you can store it.

Sweet and Hot Turkey Jerky

Ingredients:

- 2 lb. of boneless, skinless turkey breast
- ½ cup of soy sauce
- ¼ cup of brown sugar
- ¼ cup of sesame oil
- 2 tbsp of honey
- 2 tbsp of sesame seeds
- 2 tbsp of minced fresh ginger
- 1 tbsp of chipotle chili powder
- 1 tbsp of minced fresh garlic
- 2 tsp of ground black pepper

Instructions:

1. Cut the visible fat off and freeze the turkey for about an hour.
2. Cut it into 1/8th-inch thick strips.
3. Heat a tbsp of sesame oil over medium heat and cook the garlic and ginger for a minute.
4. Make the marinade with the rest of the ingredients, then stir in the garlic and ginger.
5. Add the turkey strips, stir to coat them completely, and cover the bowl. Refrigerate for four to six hours.
6. Preheat your oven to its lowest heat setting and wrap aluminum foil around baking trays.
7. Place the turkey strips on the tray, leaving a gap between them, and bake until flexible, about three to four hours. Leave the oven door open a little to let moisture out.
8. Remove the turkey strips and set them on a plate to cool down overnight.

Thanksgiving Cranberry Turkey Jerky

Ingredients:

- 2 lb. of skinless, boneless turkey breast
- 1 cup of fresh cranberries
- 1 whole fresh orange
- ¼ cup of brown sugar
- ½ cup of red wine vinegar
- 1 tbsp of minced fresh ginger

Instructions:

1. Freeze the meat for about an hour, then slice off the fat and cut the meat into strips, about 1/8th-inch thick.
2. Place the strips into a bowl and add the vinegar, ensuring the turkey is covered. Set it to one side for two hours.
3. Slice the orange into segments and grate the zest – you want 1 tbsp.
4. Add the orange segments, cranberries, ginger, and zest to a blender and blend to a puree.
5. Drain the turkey, place it in a bag or bowl, and add the fruit puree. Make sure the turkey is completely coated.
6. Preheat your oven to 190°F to 230°F and place foil over baking trays. Spread the turkey strips out over the trays, leaving a space between them, and bake for five hours, making sure the oven door is open a little.
7. Turn the turkey regularly to ensure it dries evenly. Once dried, remove and leave to cool in a dry place overnight before storing.

Fruity Punch Turkey Jerky

Ingredients:

- 2 lb. of boneless, skinless turkey meat
- ½ cup of red wine
- ¼ cup of orange juice
- ¼ cup of pineapple juice
- 1 whole garlic clove
- 2 tbsp of soy sauce

- 1 tbsp of onion powder
- 1 tbsp of minced fresh ginger
- 2 tsp of salt

Instructions:

1. Freeze the turkey for about an hour, then cut off the fat. Slice the meat into strips, about 1/8th-inch thick.
2. Make the marinade with the rest of the ingredients. Add the turkey, coat each strip all over, and put it in the fridge overnight.
3. Turn your oven to 170-190LF and line baking trays with foil.
4. Arrange the strips evenly on the trays with a gap between them. Leave the oven door open a little and dry the turkey for about four hours or until dried properly.
5. Place the jerky on a plate, leave it somewhere dry, and cool overnight to dry. Store it in an airtight container.

Fish

Before you learn how to make fish jerky, you have to know the right way to work with fish.

1. Choose Your Fish

First, you must never use pre-cooked fish for fish jerky, only raw. That's because raw fish dries out easily, and pre-cooked fish is more likely to spoil. Secondly, try to use lean fish where possible, as it takes less time to dry. That said, you can use fish like salmon, and you'll learn how to make salmon jerky later.

2. Clean and Cut It Properly

You will need a very sharp filleting knife for this. Start by removing the head and guts, followed by the bones and any excess waste. These are the parts that are likely to contain bacteria.

Wash the fish using boiled water to remove excess sea or lake water, which could also be full of bacteria. Small fish are cut differently from large fish:

- **Small:** if the fish is an inch or less thick, remove the bones and intestines and use the fish whole.
- **Large:** these must be filleted and cut into small, even-sized pieces so they dry at the same rate.

Small or large, the fish must be cleaned before processing.

3. Brine It

When you brine fish, you soak it in saltwater. Salt is one of the best-known preservatives, and it helps stop bacteria from spoiling the fish. Add salt to boiling water until it no longer dissolves – ideally, a ratio of 6 parts salt to 1 part water. Only use iodine-free salt and soak the fish for at least an hour before you begin drying it.

4. Hang It

All preservation methods require you to remove excess water so that bacteria cannot live on the meat or fish. Once your fish has been brined, you need to get rid of as much water as possible and then hang it for drying. There are three ways to dry fish:

- **Air Dry:** Hang the fish so air can circulate around it. If you live in a cold region, this probably won't work.

- **Heat Dry:** Hang the fish near a heat source to allow it to dry quickly, especially where there isn't enough air circulation. However, don't allow it to heat it so much that the fish is cooked. A dehydrator would probably be the best bet.
- **Smoke Dry:** This is the traditional method of drying fish for jerky.

When you smoke fish, you can hot or cold smoke it. You don't need to add any other preservatives if you choose hot smoked.

5. Watch It

Make sure you turn the fish regularly so it dries evenly. Warm air, good circulation, and low humidity are required to make the best jerky.

6. Store It

Like meat or poultry jerky, fish jerky also needs to be stored in a cool place in an airtight container for a long shelf life.

Time to make some jerky!

Hawaiian Fish Jerky

Ingredients:

- 2 lb. of fish fillets – tuna, snapper, trout, bass, and crappie all work well for this
- ½ cup of soy sauce
- ¼ cup of pineapple juice
- 1 tbsp of brown sugar
- 1 whole garlic clove, crushed

- 1 tbsp of minced fresh ginger
- 1 tsp of salt
- 1 tsp of ground black pepper
- ¼ tsp of cayenne pepper

Instructions:

1. Cut the fish into strips. You want them between three and six inches in length, an inch wide, and about ¼-inch thick.
2. Make the marinade by putting everything else in a resealable bag and mixing it together. Add the fish, push out the air, and seal the bag. Put it in the fridge overnight.
3. Put the fish into a colander to drain off the marinade and pat the fish dry with clean paper towels.
4. Preheat your oven to 145°F (or the lowest setting if your oven doesn't go this low), line the bottom of the oven with aluminum foil or a drip tray, and oil the top rack. You can lay the fish over the rack or thread them onto soaked skewers and suspend them so they hang down.
5. Leave the door open a little and heat for two hours. Turn the heat down to 130°F or open the oven door a bit more to cool it down. Continue heating until the fish is dry but doesn't break, and has a dark brown glaze.
6. Set the fish aside until it cools right down, then store it in the fridge in an airtight container.

Sakura Boshi

Ingredients:

- 2 lb. of ahi tuna
- 1 cup of granulated sugar
- 1 cup of shoyu
- 1-inch piece of sliced fresh ginger
- 1 tbsp of sesame seeds
- 1 tsp of minced garlic
- 1 tsp of miso paste

Instructions:

1. Cut the fish into 1/8th to ¼-inch wide strips – they should all be roughly the same thickness.
2. Mix everything else together to make the marinade.
3. Lay the slices of fish in a shallow baking dish and add the marinade.
4. Put a clean towel over the dish and put it in the fridge overnight.
5. Lift the fish from the marinade and pat as much marinade off as possible. Arrange them on the dehydrator trays with a small gap between each one.
6. Dehydrate at 160°F for five to ten hours, depending on how thick the slices are. Once done, the jerky should be a little leathery.
7. Let the fish strips cool completely before storing them.

Lemon Pepper Salmon Jerky

Ingredients:

- 1 ¼ lb. of boneless, skin-on salmon fillet
- 2/5 cup of soy sauce
- 1 tbsp of freshly squeezed lemon juice
- 1 tbsp of maple syrup
- 2 tsp of ground black pepper
- 2 tsp of liquid smoke – any
- 5 ½ tbsp of coarse sea salt

Instructions:

1. Get the pin bones out of the fish – use a sharp knife or ask the fishmonger to do it.
2. Take the silver flesh off the top, but do not remove the skin.
3. Wash and dry the fish and freeze it for half an hour.
4. Cut the fish into slices about a cm thick.
5. Put the soy sauce, lemon juice, pepper sauce, liquid smoke, pepper, and maple syrup in a large bowl and mix it thoroughly.
6. Add the fish, making sure each piece is coated all over. Cover the dish and put it in the fridge. Marinate overnight – at least 12 hours.
7. Drain the salmon, discard the marinade, and pat the excess off the fish.

8. Place a clean wire rack over a foil-covered baking tray and lay the fish pieces on it. Sprinkel salt over both sides of the fish and refrigerate for 2 hours.
9. Preheat your oven to 167°F and place a silicon baking mat or baking paper over a baking tray.
10. Brush the salt off the fish and lay the pieces on the tray, leaving a gap between them.
11. Cook until a meat thermometer inserted in the fish reads 167°F, then reduce the temperature to 140°F. Continue cooking, turning the pieces halfway through, until the jerky is sticky and chewy inside with a crisp outer shell. It should take about 4 ½ hours in total.
12. Allow the fish to cool completely before storing it.

Trout Jerky

Ingredients:

- 1 lb. of trout fillet
- ¼ cup of soy sauce
- 1 tbsp of light brown sugar
- 1 tsp of minced fresh garlic
- 1 tsp of olive oil
- ½ tsp of ground black pepper

Instructions:

1. Cut the fish into slices about an inch wide.
2. Put the olive oil and soy sauce in a small pan, add the garlic, pepper, and sugar, and heat it over low heat. Whisk constantly until the sugar has dissolved, then

take the pan off the heat. Set it aside until it has cooled to room temperature.

3. Pour the marinade into a sealable bag, add the fish, and seal it, removing as much air as possible. Put it in the fridge for at least four hours, no more than eight.

4. Lift the fish pieces and use clean paper towels to remove as much marinade as possible.

5. If you are dehydrating the fish, set the dehydrator to 160°F. If using the oven, set it to 150°F. It can take up to 12 hours if you are drying the fish in the oven, and you'll need to watch it closely to make sure it doesn't burn.

6. Place the strips a little apart on oven or dehydrator racks

7. Cook until the strips are chewy and leathery, checking them after four to six hours.

8. Once cooked, let them cool at room temperature before storing them.

Honey-Miso Salmon Jerky

Ingredients:

- 3 lb. of salmon fillet
- 5 tbsp of honey
- 5 tbsp of soy sauce
- 3 tbsp of seasoned rice wine vinegar
- 3 tbsp of white miso
- 3 tbsp of sesame seeds
- 2 tbsp of sesame oil

- 3 tsp of garlic powder
- 3 tsp of freshly cracked black pepper
- 1 ½ tsp of crushed red pepper flakes
- 1 ½ tsp of ginger powder

Instructions:

1. Wrap the salmon and freeze it for 15 to 30 minutes, until firm enough to slice easily but not frozen.
2. Mix the remaining ingredients in a large Ziploc bag until thoroughly combined and the honey has dissolved.
3. Remove any skin from the salmon. If it is a whole fillet, cut it in half lengthwise, then slice it into 1/8-inch thick strips against the grain.
4. Add the fish slices to the bag with the marinade, ensuring each piece is coated. Remove the air from the bag, seal it, and refrigerate for eight to 24 hours – 16 hours is about right, but longer won't hurt. Rotate the bag a few times throughout the marinating time.
5. Heat your smoker, oven, or dehydrator to 165°F. If your oven doesn't go that low, open the oven door a little.
6. Place aluminum foil on baking sheets and put wire racks on them.
7. Drain the fish and pat the excess marinade off. Place the fish in a single layer in your chosen cooking utensil and cook for three to six hours. If you are using your oven, change the trays over and turn them around after two hours.
8. At three hours, you can start checking the jerky.

9. Once cooked, set it aside to cool completely, then store it in an airtight container.

Teriyaki Tuna Jerky

Ingredients:

- 2 lb. of raw tuna fillet
- ¾ cup of teriyaki sauce
- ½ cup of soy sauce
- 1 minced garlic clove
- 4 tbsp of sugar
- 2 tsp of grated fresh ginger

Instructions:

1. Freeze the tuna for an hour or two before cutting it into slices about 1/8th to ½-inch thick.
2. Make the marinade with the remaining ingredients. Place the tuna slices in a shallow dish, pour the marinade over, and stir to make sure each piece is coated. Cover the dish and put it in the fridge overnight.
3. Set your oven to 145-15°F and place foil over a baking sheet. Place a rack on it and lay the tuna slices in an even layer, not touching.
4. Back for six hours, flipping the pieces halfway through.
5. When the tuna has reached the consistency you want, remove it and let it cool down completely before storing it.

Tilapia Jerky

Ingredients:

- 2 lb. of tilapia fillets
- 1 cup of brown sugar
- ½ cup of soy sauce
- 2 tbsp of molasses
- 1 tbsp of lemon juice
- 2 tsp of liquid smoke
- 1 tsp of Worcestershire sauce

Instructions:

1. Freeze the tilapia for up to half an hour before slicing it into 1/8-inch thick strips.
2. Combine the marinade ingredients in a large Ziploc bag and place the fish in it. Massage it to coat all the fish pieces, remove the air, and seal the bag. Refrigerate for eight hours.
3. Set your dehydrator to preheat to its lowest temperature. Drain the fish and remove as much excess marinade as you can with clean paper towels.
4. Lay the fish on the dehydrator trays and let them dry out for six to eight hours.
5. When they are dried to your liking, set them aside to cool before storing them somewhere cool and dry.

Spicy Salmon Jerky

Ingredients:

- 3 lb. of skinless salmon fillet
- 1 cup of soy sauce
- 2 tbsp of white sugar
- 2 tbsp of molasses
- 2 tbsp of lemon juice
- 2 tbsp of Worcestershire sauce
- 2 tsp of liquid smoke
- 1 ½ tsp of ground black pepper
- 1 ½ tsp of hot sauce

Instructions:

1. Slice the salmon into four equal bits widthwise. Turn each piece one turn 90 degrees and slice it lengthwise into pieces about ¼-inch thick. Get the pin bones out using needle-nose pliers. Do not cut into the bony bits in the middle.
2. Mix the marinade ingredients in a bowl and put the salmon strips in. Make sure each piece is coated, cover the bowl, and place it in the refrigerator for about four hours.
3. Drain the salmon and use clean paper towels to pat the salmon dry.
4. Lay the strips in your dehydrator and leave them at the lowest heat setting for about six hours.

5. Check every couple of hours, and when they are done to your liking, remove them and let them cool down completely.

Spicy Trout Jerky

Ingredients:

- 1 lb. of trout fillets
- 1/3 cup of cold water
- ½ tsp of kosher salt
- ½ tsp of garlic powder
- ½ tsp of onion powder
- ½ tsp of cayenne pepper
- ¼ tsp of curing salt – OPTIONAL
- ¼ tsp of chipotle chili powder

Instructions:

1. Remove the scales from the trout using a butter knife. Work from the tail up to the head.
2. Fillet the trout, giving you two pieces per fish. Remove the pin and rib bones, but leave the skin on. Run cold water over them.
3. Cut each piece into strips about four to five inches long and ¼-1/2-inch thick.
4. Make the marinade in a sealable bag and add the fish pieces. Massage gently to coat all the fish, squeeze out as much air as you can, and then seal the bag. Refrigerate for six to 24 hours.

5. Preheat your dehydrator to 150°F. Drain the fish and pat off the excess liquid.

6. Dry the fish on the racks for four hours until they are bendy, but do not break.

7. If you want to use your oven, set it at its lowest temperature and leave the door open a little. Dry the fish for about four hours.

8. Remove the fish from the oven or dehydrator and set it aside on a plate to cool. Before you eat or store the fish, peel off the skin.

Other Meats

Goose or Duck Jerky

Ingredients

- 3 lb. skinless goose or duck breast
- 2 cups of water
- ¼ cup of Worcestershire sauce
- 3 tbsp of brown sugar
- 2 tbsp of kosher salt
- 1 tsp of cayenne
- 1 tsp of dried thyme
- 1 tsp of garlic powder
- 1 tsp of porcini powder - OPTIONAL
- ½ tsp of Instacure #1 – OPTIONAL

Instructions:

1. Put the goose or duck into the freezer and cool it for an hour or two. Slice off the fat and cut the meat into pieces about ¼-inch thick.

2. Make the marinade with the rest of the ingredients in a resealable bag or a shallow dish. Add the meat, massage to coat it, and refrigerate for 24 to 72 hours. The longer you leave it, the saltier it will be, but it will have a better flavor. Massage the meat occasionally to make sure it stays coated in marinade.

3. Lift the meat and pat off the excess marinade with paper towels. Place the pieces on the dehydrator trays and dry them for four to six hours at 140°F.

4. If you prefer to use the oven, set it to the lowest heat setting and dry the fish for four to six hours, or until it is pliable but dry.

5. Let the jerky cool right down before you store it.

Spicy Goose Jerky

Ingredients:

- 4 lb. of goose breast fillets, skinless and trimmed of all fat and silver skin
- 1 cup of brown sugar
- 1 cup of water
- ¾ cup of soy sauce
- ¼ cup of Worcestershire sauce
- 3 tbsp of coarse sea salt
- 3 tbsp of coarse ground black pepper

- 2 tbsp of crushed red pepper flakes
- 2 tbsp of chili powder
- 2 tbsp of garlic powder

Instructions:

1. Put the meat in the freezer for a couple of hours, then cut off the gat. Slice the meat into ¼-inch strips, with the grain for chewy jerky and against it for soft, tender jerky. You can tenderize it even more by using a meat mallet to pound the meat.

2. Mix the rest of the ingredients and place the goose breast in it. Make sure each piece is coated before covering the dish and putting it in the fridge for at least 12 hours, up to 24.

3. Drain the meat and pat the excess marinade off with clean paper towels. Arrange them on a baking rack and put them in the fridge for one hour.

4. Set your oven or smoker to 175°F and arrange the meat in a single layer on the racks. Heat for about an hour or until the meat is 165°F inside – use a meat thermometer.

5. Turn the temperature down to 140°F (if using an oven, leave the door open a little or open all the smoker vents) and heat for five hours. Flip the strips over and dry for another five hours, or until done to your preference.

6. Let the jerky cool completely before you store it.

Rabbit Jerky

Ingredients:

- 2 lb. of fresh rabbit meat
- ½ cup of soy sauce
- ½ cup of Worcestershire sauce
- 1 tsp of garlic powder
- 1 tsp of seasoning salt
- 1 tsp of onion powder
- 1 tsp of ground black pepper

Instructions:

1. Cut the rabbit into strips – the thinner they are, the quicker they will dry.
2. Make the marinade and submerge the strips of rabbit in it, making sure each piece is completely coated. Cover and refrigerate for 12 to 24 hours.
3. Preheat your oven to 250°F and place a sheet of aluminum on a baking sheet.
4. Drain the meat and place the strips on an oven rack, leaving a gap between each one to let the air circulate.
5. Heat for four to six hours, depending on the size of the strips, but you will need to remove any moisture every hour. You can do this by reducing the heat to 160°F after three hours and turning the strips over every hour.
6. If using a smoker, open the vents every hour for a few minutes.

7. Once the meat is fully dry, remove it and let it cool at room temperature.

Orange-Soy-Ginger Rabbit-Belly Jerky

Ingredients:

- 10 to 12 rabbit belly flaps
- 1 cup of soy sauce
- 1 cup of orange juice
- ½ cup of honey
- 1 tbsp of ground black pepper
- 1 tsp of grated fresh ginger
- 1 tsp of cayenne pepper
- ½ tsp of Instacure # 1

Instructions:

1. Slice the bellies into slices the size you want the jerky to be, trimming any fat off.
2. Mix the marinade ingredients and place the rabbit slices in it. Mix and refrigerate for six to 12 hours.
3. Preheat your dehydrator or smoker to 160°F. Drain the meat, pat off any extra marinade, lay the strips on the dehydrator or smoker racks, and heat for about six hours or until fully dry. Flip the strips over about halfway through the cooking time.
4. Once dried, cool completely and store.

Deer Jerky

Ingredients:

- 1 lb. of venison roast, boneless
- 4 tbsp of Worcestershire sauce
- 4 tbsp of soy sauce
- 2 tbsp of liquid smoke
- 1 tbsp of ketchup
- ½ tsp of salt
- ¼ tsp of garlic powder
- ¼ tsp of black pepper
- ¼ tsp of onion salt

Instructions:

1. Freeze the meat for about an hour but only until firm, not frozen.
2. Make the marinade in a sealable bag or large bowl. Cut the venison into strips about an inch wide and 1/8th inch thick. Put them into the marinade. Massage to coat the venison, cover, and refrigerate for at least eight hours, preferably overnight. Massage the bag or stir the container to ensure the venison stays in the marinade.
3. Preheat your oven to 160°F and lay a sheet of aluminum foil or a baking tray at the bottom.
4. Drain the venison, pat off the marinade, and lay the strips in a wire rack. Dry for six to eight hours or until they are done to your liking.

5. Let them cool down completely and store.

Sweet and Spicy Venison Jerky

Ingredients:

- 1 lb. of venison
- ½ cup of Worcestershire sauce
- ½ cup of teriyaki sauce
- ½ cup of brown sugar
- 1/3 cup of soy sauce
- 3 tbsp of liquid smoke
- 1 tbsp of lemon juice
- 1 tbsp of garlic salt
- 1 tbsp of onion powder
- 1 tbsp of ground black pepper
- 1 tsp of hot pepper sauce
- 1 tsp of paprika

Instructions:

1. Place all the ingredients except the venison in a large bowl and whisk together.
2. Firm the venison up in the freezer and then cut into strips about ¼-inch thick.
3. Add the venison strips to the marinade. Make sure they are fully coated, cover the dish, and put it in the fridge for 24 hours. Stir it once or twice during this time.

4. Lift the venison from the marinade, pat it dry, and arrange it on your dehydrator trays in one layer, not touching. Turn the dehydrator to HIGH and heat for about four hours or until pliable but dry.

5. If you prefer, you can use your oven. Preheat it to 160°F, line the bottom with foil, and lay the venison strips on a wire rack. Dry the venison for six to eight hours, or until it is done to your preference. Check it after three hours, remove any strips already dried, and check it regularly thereafter.

6. Set the dried jerky to one side to cool off, and then store it.

Alligator or Crocodile Jerky

Ingredients:

- 4 lb. of alligator or crocodile meat
- 1 ¼ cup of Worcestershire sauce
- ¾ cup of soy sauce
- ½ cup of brown sugar
- ½ cup of liquid smoke
- 3 tbsp of onion powder
- 1 tbsp of cayenne pepper
- 3 tsp of salt

Instructions:

1. Cut off as much external fat as possible, before cutting the meat into slices about 1/8th-inch thick. You can freeze the meat for about an hour first, if you want, to make slicing it easier.

2. Make the marinade by heating the rest of the ingredients in a pan over low heat, stirring constantly to dissolve the sugar. When you have a smooth sauce, take the pan off the heat and set it aside to cool.

3. Put the meat into a bowl, add the marinade, and coat each strip in it. Put the bowl in the fridge overnight.

4. Preheat your oven to its lowest heat settings and place aluminum foil over a couple of baking sheets.

5. Pour the meat into a colander to drain off the marinade. Use paper towels to clean off the excess and arrange the strips on baking trays, in one layer and not touching each other.

6. Leave the oven door open a little so moisture can escape, and dry the meat for around four to six hours until flexible but snappy.

7. Pat off any moisture and let the meat cool down before storing.

Ostrich or Emu Jerky

Ingredients:

- 1 ½ lb. of ostrich or emu meat
- ¼ cup of dark soy sauce
- 2 tbsp of Worcestershire sauce
- 1 tbsp of apple cider vinegar
- 1 tsp of onion powder
- 1 tsp of hot sauce
- 1 tsp of garlic powder
- ½ tsp of ground ginger

Instructions:

1. Cut off the gristle or fat and put the meat in the freezer for about an hour.
2. Cut into ½-inch thick slices.
3. Mix all the marinade ingredients and place the meat in it. Stir to coat and set aside for four hours or more. Soak bamboo skewers in cold water.
4. Preheat your oven to its lowest heat, between 190°F and 230°F.
5. Drain the meat, remove any excess marinade, and thread the strips onto soaked skewers. Hang them across your oven racks and place a tray at the bottom to catch the drips.
6. Cook with the oven door propped open a little for about six hours until tender but flexible.
7. Set the jerky aside overnight to cool down before you store it.

Kangaroo Jerky

Ingredients:

- 2 lb. of kangaroo steak
- 1/3 cup of soy sauce
- 2 tbsp of hickory smoked sea salt
- 2 tbsp of Worcestershire sauce
- 1 tsp of hot sauce
- 1 tsp of pepper
- 1 tsp of garlic powder

- ½ tsp of onion powder

Instructions:

1. Put the meat in the freezer for an hour before slicing it into 1/8th-inch thick strips along the grain.
2. Rub the salt all over the meat and set it aside for one hour.
3. Mix the remaining ingredients and place the kangaroo in it. Mix and refrigerate overnight.
4. Preheat your oven to the lowest temperature and wrap the racks in foil.
5. Place a sheet of foil at the bottom of the oven and lay the meat over the racks.
6. Prop the oven door open a bit and dry the jerky for three to four hours.
7. Pat the excess moisture off the jerky and let it cool down.

Lamb Jerky

Ingredients:

- 1 lb. of lean lamb
- 3 tbsp of soy sauce
- 2 tbsp of liquid smoke
- 1 tbsp garlic powder
- 1 tbsp minced fresh garlic
- 1 tbsp of onion powder
- ½ tbsp of Tabasco sauce

Instructions:

1. Put the lamb in the freezer for no more than two hours before cutting the external fat off and slicing the meat into strips about ¼-inch thick.
2. Make the marinade in a shallow dish and add the lamb. Stir to coat each piece and put a cover over the bowl. Set it aside overnight.
3. Set your oven to its lowest temperature and line the racks with foil.
4. Lift the lamb from the marinade and pat off the excess. Put the strips onto the covered racks.
5. Leave the door open a little and heat for four hours until the meat starts curling and it has the right consistency.
6. Take the meat out of the oven, pat it dry with clean paper towels, and set aside to cool overnight before storing.

Sweet Maple Pork Jerky

Ingredients:

- 1 lb. of pork tenderloin
- 2 cups of brown sugar
- ¼ cup of maple syrup
- ¼ cup of cold water
- 1 ½ tsp of sea salt
- ¼ tsp of curing salt – OPTIONAL

Instructions:

1. Cut the fat off the pork, wrap the meat in plastic wrap, and put it in the freezer for up to two hours.
2. Mix the marinade ingredients in a bowl or sealable bag.
3. Cut the meat into strips about ¼-inch thick. Cutt it with or against the grain, depending on how you want the jerky.
4. Add the meat to the marinade and put it in the fridge for eight to 24 hours.
5. Remove the meat from the marinade, pat it dry, and dry it at 165°F using your preferred method.
6. Let the jerky cool right down before you store it.

Vegan/Vegetarian
Tofu Jerky

Ingredients:

- 1 lb. of extra firm tofu
- ½ cup of soy sauce
- ¼ cup of dark beer or water
- 3 tbsp of liquid smoke
- 1 tbsp of fresh ground black pepper
- 1 tbsp of onion powder
- 1 tsp of garlic powder OR one fresh clove, minced
- 1 tsp of maple syrup or honey

Instructions:

1. Drain the tofu, removing all excess liquid. Cutting on the short side, slice it into long, thin strips, about four to five mm thick.
2. Mix the marinade ingredients. Lay the tofu in a single layer in a shallow dish or baking pan and pour the marinade over. Leave it overnight.
3. Drain the marinade and place the strips on your dehydrator trays or in an oven preheated to 200°F. Dry for four to eight hours until chewy and no longer white. Turn the tofu over a few times during cooking to ensure even drying.
4. Take the tofu out of the dehydrator and set it aside to cool. Then store it in an airtight container.

Variations:

Add the following ingredients to change the flavor of your marinade:

- **Chili:** add a little chili powder
- **Spicy:** a little cayenne pepper or Tabasco sauce
- **Pizza:** a little dried basil and oregano

Eggplant Jerky

Ingredients:

- 1 large eggplant, approximately 1 lb.
- ½ cup of olive oil
- 4 tbsp of balsamic vinegar
- 2 tbsp of maple syrup

- ½ tsp of paprika
- Salt – regular or applewood-smoked

Instructions:

1. Clean the eggplant, dry it, and slice it into long strips, all an even thickness.
2. Make the marinade in a large bowl and coat the eggplant strips in it. Marinate it for two hours.
3. Preheat your oven to the lowest setting and line the baking sheets with baking paper. Place the eggplant strips on it, sprinkle with a little salt, and bake for 10 to 12 hours or until crisp and dry. Turn the eggplant halfway through cooking and blot off any oil you see.
4. If using your dehydrator, place the eggplant strips on the trays and put another solid tray at the bottom to catch the drips. Sprinkle salt over the eggplant and dry for 12 to 18 hours at 115°F until crisp and dry.
5. Let the jerky strips cool down, and then you can store them.

Beet Jerky

Ingredients:

- 1 ½ lb. of trimmed, cleaned beets
- ¼ cup of vegan Worcestershire sauce
- ¼ cup of tamari sauce
- 1 tsp of ground pepper
- 1 tsp of maple syrup
- ½ tsp of garlic powder

- ½ tsp of onion powder

Instructions:

1. Cut the beets into strips about 1/8th inch thick. A mandolin is the best wat to do this.
2. Whisk the marinade ingredients and add the beets. Stir to make sure they are coated all over, and put the bowl in the fridge for two hours up to two days.
3. Preheat your oven to 200°F, and place racks in the bottom and middle sections. Place a sheet of baking paper on two baking sheets.
4. Drain the marinade and lay the beets on the baking sheets, not overlapping.
5. Bake until the moisture is gone and the beets are pliable but dry, about 2 ½ to 2 ¾ hours.
6. Remove, let them cool completely, and store.

Sesame Maple Tempeh Jerky

Ingredients:

- 8 ounces of gluten-free tempeh
- ¼ cup of gluten-free soy sauce
- 3 tbsp of maple syrup or coconut nectar
- 2 tbsp of sesame seeds
- 2 tbsp of water
- 1 tsp of toasted sesame oil
- ¼ tsp of liquid smoke
- ¼ tsp of ground ginger

- 1/8 tsp of garlic powder
- 1/8 tsp of cayenne pepper

Instructions:

1. Add a cup of water to a pan, bring it to a boil, and put the tempeh in. Let it simmer for a couple of minutes, before flipping the tempeh and cooking for one or two minutes. Lift the tempeh, dry it using paper towels, and set it on a clean cutting board.
2. Slice the tempeh into strips about ¼-inch wide. Slice each strip into 16 little triangular pieces.
3. Make the marinade with the rest of the ingredients (leave the sesame seeds out_ and set it to one side.
4. Put the tempeh triangles in a shallow dish and add the marinade. Turn the tempeh so it is covered on all sides, and cover the dish. Refrigerate for 12 hours or more, turning the pieces a couple of times to ensure they absorb the liquid all over.
5. Preheat your oven to 350°F and put a rack in the center. Line a baking sheet with parchment paper. Pour the tempeh into a colander to drain the marinade into a bowl (reserve for later) and then lay them on the baking sheet. Sprinkle half the sesame seeds over them, turn the pieces over, and add the rest of the seeds.
6. Bake the tempeh for about 15 minutes. Flip them, and spoon the marinade over the top. Bake for 5 minutes until they are golden brown, turning again if needed to stop it from burning.
7. Remove and eat it warm or cool it and store it for up to three days in the refrigerator.

Shiitake Mushroom Jerky

Ingredients:

- 8 ounces of destemmed shiitake mushrooms
- ¼ cup of soy sauce or coconut aminos
- 2 tbsp of apple cider vinegar
- 1 tbsp of garlic chili paste
- ¼ tsp of smoked paprika
- 1/8 tsp of black pepper

Instructions:

1. Put the chili paste, soy sauce or aminos, pepper, vinegar, and paprika in a sealable bag and mix it all up. Cut the mushrooms into thin slices and put them in the bag. Toss to coat each slice and put them in the fridge overnight.
2. Set your oven to 250°F and line a baking sheet with parchment paper. Lift the mushroom slices on to the sheet using tongs, making sure the excess marinade drips off first. Leave a gap between each slice.
3. Bake them for an hour, flip the mushrooms over, and cook for 35 to 45 minutes, depending on their size.
4. When they are done, the mushrooms will look dry and shrunken. Allow them to cool fully before you store them.

Fruit Jerky

Ingredients:

- Your choice of fruit – must be ripe or overripe but not off
- Lime juice
- Lemon juice
- Sugar syrup

Instructions:

1. Peel the fruit and get rid of any stones or seeds. Cut the fruit into little pieces and put it in a blender. Puree it. When you choose the amount of fruit to use, remember that your finished jerky will be one-quarter of what you started with.
2. If you use sweet fruits, add 1 tsp of lemon or lime juice per quart of puree. If using tarter fruits, add 1 tsp of sugar syrup per quart.
3. Place baking paper on a shallow baking tray and pour the puree on it. Distribute it evenly.
4. Preheat your oven to 200°F and bake the fruit puree for about four hours, or until it reaches the texture you want. Leave the oven door open a little.
5. Let it cool, slice it, and store it.

Chapter 6: Flavorful Jerky Marinades and Seasonings

Marinades do more than look good. Depending on the ingredients, they add moisture and flavor to virtually any food. Using salt in a marinade helps the flavors penetrate beneath the surface and dig deep into the rest of the meat, fish, or whatever else you are marinating.

17. Marinades can add moisture and flavor to almost any food. Source: https://unsplash.com/photos/a-bowl-of-olive-oil-and-a-fork-m75X_lLg7ec?utm_content=creditShareLink&utm_medium=referral&utm_source=unsplash

This chapter discusses how marinades work, how to make them, and a few recipes to get you started.

How Do Marinades Work?

When meat, fish, or other foodstuff is marinated, it is soaked in a seasoned liquid, usually acidic. That liquid is flavored with herbs and spices, and the acid – vinegar, citrus, fruit enzymes, etc. – helps break down the surface of the food and change its texture and flavors.

These acids work on the surface of the food, but using too much or soaking the food for too long. If you do, the food can get to dry and tough or turn to mush. The right blend of acid, oil, and seasonings is critical for a truly great marinade.

Marinades only go a little way into the meat or fish when you soak it, which is why it works really well for thin slices, like jerky. For example, if you use ginger, honey, and soy sauce, the ginger and honey stay on the food's surface, while the salt in the soy sauce goes into the center of the food.

Salt draws the liquid out of the food using osmosis, breaking down the muscle fibers and allowing the brine to be easily absorbed. The brine carries garlic, onion, or any other water-soluble ingredient into the meat, and the oils carry fat-soluble ingredients, like herbs, spices, and chili, onto the surface of the food.

Benefits of Marinating Meat

Marinating your food offers three main benefits:

1. **Taste and Flavor:** Marinades allow you to get creative and use pretty much any ingredients you want to give your jerky some cool flavors. Make your jerk herby, spicy, smoky, or sweet.

2. **Texture:** Marinades can make your meat juicy and tender and are great for tougher cuts of meat.

3. **Moisture and Tenderness:** In the same way that brining does, marinating adds moisture to meat that would normally dry out when cooked. Where brine uses salt, marinades use oils, sugar, spices, herbs, and other seasonings to bring flavor and tenderness to whatever you are cooking.

Basic Marinade Ingredients

Making a good marinade is as easy as throwing some ingredients in a bowl and whisking them together. However, there are some rules to follow and certain types of ingredients you should include, so long as you get the balance right:

- **Fat:** Fat is a vital ingredient in any marinade, as it is the only way to get herbs, spices, and other fat-soluble ingredients into the meat or fish. Not only that, but it also helps the food stay moist. Fat goes really well with some flavors. It can help sharp, acidic flavors mellow a little and blend with the rest of the ingredients, and you could use tahini, buttermilk, oil (including flavored), yogurt, etc.

- **Salt:** Salt is also vital, as it helps the water-soluble flavors penetrate beyond the outer surface of the food. Salt also breaks the food's protein structure down, making extra space for more moisture. Salt is critical when you need to marinate tough cuts of meat. That's because it tenderizes the meat by breaking the muscle fibers down. You can use sea salt, soy sauce, fish sauce, seasoned salt, pickle juice, or vinegar to add salt.

- **Acid:** Acid does two jobs. First, it helps the proteins on the surface of the food loosen up, and second, it helps improve the flavor. There are loads of different acids you can use, including pickle juice, hot sauce, buttermilk, vinegar, citrus juice, etc.
- **Enzymes:** These get to work on the connective tissues lining the surface of the meat, heling break them down so the brine and other flavors can penetrate. Usually, these would come from pineapple, papaya, and some other fruits.
- **Seasonings:** These add real flavor to the marinade. If you mix seasonings to make dry rubs, add these to the rest of the ingredients to make a beautiful marinade. Use ingredients like red pepper, black pepper, chili powder, curry powder, curry paste, mustard, garlic, ginger, Worcestershire sauce, and more.
- **Herbs:** Fresh or dried herbs boost any marinade's flavor and health benefits. Some of the best ones are dill, basil, oregano, sage, parsley, tarragon, and thyme.
- **Sugar:** Sweet ingredients add a certain level of complexity and can be added in the form of molasses, honey, white or brown sugar, barbecue sauce, ketchup, and so on.

Marinade Tips

Although marinades can take your meat, fish, or veggies to another level, and the ingredients are only bounded by your imagination and creativity, there are some things you must remember:

18. Marinating certain food can take a long time. Source: https://unsplash.com/photos/a-bowl-of-olive-oil-and-a-fork-m75X_lLg7ec?utm_content=creditShareLink&utm_medium=referral&utm_source=unsplash

- **Time:** While it doesn't take long to make a marinade, marinating certain food can take a long time, while others must only be marinated for a short time. Pay close attention to the recipe instructions, and never leave food in a marinade for too long, or it will break down and become tough or mushy.

- **Acid:** While acid is a necessary ingredient, adding too much will toughen meat or poultry, drying it out. That means using the right balance of fat, sugar, salt, and acid is crucial. If you use too much acid, it can "cook" seafood, shellfish, and other delicate foods.

- **Sugar:** When a marinade recipe asks for a sweet ingredient, you need to remember that it will burn quicker than a marinade without it. Monitor the food carefully to make sure it doesn't char.

Marinating Your Meat Safely

Poultry, raw seafood, pork, and other meats can have bacteria in them that can get into the marinade and contaminate it. Because of that, certain precautions must be taken:

- **Use the Refrigerator:** Unless otherwise stated, food should always be marinated in the refrigerator, as the cold will slow or stop the growth of bacteria.

- **Never Reuse Marinades:** If your marinade would make a lovely sauce for another recipe, make some extra. You should never use any marinade that has had food soaked in it, as there is a high risk of cross-contamination. If you make extra, store it way from the marinade being used for the jerky.

- **Non-Reactive Materials:** Always make your marinades in containers that are non-reactive, i.e., glass or food-safe plastic. Marinades contain acids that can react with other materials, like metal, ceramic, etc. Do not use aluminum foil or aluminum cooking dishes.

How Long Should Food Be Marinated For?

Much of that depends on the marinade, but you can marinate foods for 30 minutes to a day or more. However, vegetables should only be marinated for a short time. Meat should not be left in marinade any longer than the recipe suggests as it can break down or toughen up, especially some fish and seafood.

- **Seafood:** Marinate shellfish and fish for 30 to 60 minutes. Any longer, the acid can start to "cook" the meat, and it can become mushy.

- **Chicken:** Remove the skin and chop the chicken into small pieces so the marinade can be better absorbed. Poultry can stay in a marinade safely for up to two days so long as it is kept refrigerated. However, two hours is typically long enough.

- **Pork and Beef:** Marinades are great for softening tough beef cuts and also for cubed pork loin and tenderloin. All of these cuts can stay in the marinade for up to 24 hours. Avoid using prime cuts of beef and steak, as some marinades can ruin them.

- **Tofu:** Tofu is wonderful at absorbing flavors and can be left marinating for up to 24 hours.

- **Vegetables:** Soft vegetables should not be marinated for more than 10 minutes as they release water and can end up soggy. Potatoes, carrots, and other harder vegetables can be marinated for up to half an hour.

Preparing Food

- **Size:** It's best to use thinner, flat meat if possible. If you can only get larger cuts, chop the into even-sized cubes or strips or slice it as thin as possible.

- **Skewers:** Small pieces of meat, fish slices, and shrimp are well threaded onto skewers and hung from the top part of the oven or smoker. This ensures they cook evenly, and you don't have to worry about turning them over so they don't burn.

Marinating Tools

- **Resealable Food Bags**: Ziploc bags are mess-free when it comes to marinating. The meat or fish is soaked right in it, and you don't need to get your hands dirty to mix it all up.

- **Skewers**: Wooden skewers make drying meat easy. Soak them in water for 20 minutes or so before you use them, or they may burn. You can use metal skewers without doing this.
- **Whisk**: Use a stainless steel whisk to combine all your marinade ingredients.
- **Bowls**: You'll need various sizes of bowls, as you'll be marinating food with varying weights. Stainless steel, glass, and food-safe plastic are the best choices as they do not react with the acid in the marinade like other materials do.
- **Baking Dish**: If you are marinating large foods, use a glass baking or casserole dish. These have enough space to ensure the food is not overcrowded and can stay in contact with the marinade.

Marinade Recipes

These are just a few ideas for marinades, just so you can see how the ingredients work together. When you are happy with making these, experiment with different ingredients. Just make sure you maintain the right flavor balance.

Beef

Basic Beef Marinade

- 2/3 cup of soy sauce
- 2/3 cup of Worcestershire sauce
- 1 tbsp of honey

- 2 tsp of onion powder
- 2 tsp of ground black pepper
- 1 tsp of red pepper flakes
- 1 tsp liquid smoke

Cajun Marinade

- 3 cups of water
- 1 cup of Worcestershire sauce
- ½ cup of soy sauce
- ¼ cup of teriyaki sauce
- 1 tbsp of onion powder
- 1 tbsp of garlic powder
- 1 tbsp of liquid smoke
- 1 tbsp of shrimp or crab boil

Pastrami Marinade

- ½ cup of soy sauce
- ½ cup of Worcestershire sauce
- ¼ cup of brown sugar
- 2 tbsp of cracked black pepper
- 2 tbsp of coriander seed
- ½ tbsp garlic puree

Hot and Spicy Marinade

- 1 cup of sweet apple cider

- ½ cup of balsamic vinegar
- ¼ cup of unpasteurized honey
- ¼ cup of Dijon mustard
- 3 tbsp of garlic powder
- 3 tbsp of sesame oil
- 2 tbsp of crushed chili pepper flakes
- 2 tbsp of fish sauce
- 2 tbsp of liquid smoke
- 2 tbsp of paprika
- 2 tbsp of cracked black pepper
- 1 tbsp of salt
- 1 tbsp of onion powder
- ¼ tsp of ground clove
- 2 chopped dried chipotle peppers

Pepper Marinade

- ¾ cup of water
- ¾ cup of soy sauce
- ¾ cup of Worcestershire sauce
- 1 ½ tbsp of brown sugar
- 1 tbsp of onion powder
- 1 tbsp of garlic powder
- 1 tbsp of liquid smoke
- 1 tbsp of ground black pepper

- ¼ tsp of cayenne pepper
- ¼ tsp of coriander seeds

Mongolian Marinade

- 4 cups of soy or tamari sauce
- 1 cup of light brown sugar
- 4 tbsp of minced fresh garlic
- 4 tbsp of minced fresh garlic
- 1 tbsp of ground black pepper
- 1 tbsp of sesame oil
- Sesame seeds for garnish

Bourbon Marinade

- 2 cups of cream soda
- 1 cup of bourbon
- ½ cup of brown sugar
- 1/3 cup of maple syrup
- ¼ cup of liquid smoke
- ¼ cup of soy sauce
- 1 tbsp of onion powder
- ½ tsp of chili powder

Buffalo-Style Marinade

- ½ cup of soy sauce
- ¼ cup of honey

- 1 ½ tbsp of crushed red pepper flakes
- 1 tbsp of grated fresh ginger
- 6 whole garlic cloves, minced

Jalapeno Sauce

- ½ cup of soy sauce
- ¼ cup of Worcestershire sauce
- ¼ cup of honey
- ¼ cup of maple syrup
- 4 tbsp of lemon juice
- 2 tbsp of garlic powder
- 2 shots of tequila
- 3 whole jalapeno peppers

Sweet Sriracha Marinade

- ½ cup of unseasoned rice wine vinegar
- ½ cup + 2 tbsp of sriracha sauce
- ¼ cup of brown sugar
- 3 tsp of ground ginger
- 1 tsp of garlic powder
- 1 tsp of salt

Chili Lime Marinade

- 2 tbsp of chili garlic sauce
- 1 ½ tbsp of lime juice

- 1 tbsp of Worcestershire sauce
- 1 tbsp of soy sauce
- 1 tbsp of brown sugar
- 1 tsp of liquid smoke – only if not smoking the jerky
- Zest from a whole lime

Korean Sauce

- 3 tbsp of soy sauce
- 3 tbsp of brown sugar
- 1 tsp of onion powder
- 1 tsp of garlic powder
- 1 tsp of Asian sesame oil

Chicken

Basic Chicken Marinade

- 2 tbsp of gourmet sauce
- 2 tbsp of Worcestershire sauce
- 1 tbsp of brown sugar
- 1 tbsp of minced fresh ginger
- 1 tbsp of salt
- 2 minced garlic cloves
- 1 tsp of paprika
- ¼ tsp of onion powder
- ¼ tsp of dried red pepper flakes

Spicy Chicken Marinade

- 2 ¼ tsp of curing salt
- 2 ¼ tsp of pickling salt
- 1 tsp of crushed red pepper flakes
- ½ tsp of cayenne pepper
- ¼ tsp of white pepper
- ¼ tsp of black pepper
- 1/8 tsp of garlic powder
- 1/8 tsp of onion powder

Honey Barbecue Marinade

- ¾ cup of honey
- ½ cup of ketchup
- ¼ cup of butter
- 2 tbsp of brown sugar
- 1 tbsp of vinegar
- 1 tbsp of soy sauce
- 2 tsp of Dijon mustard
- 1 whole garlic clove, minced
- Chili powder - OPTIONAL

Buffalo Wing Chicken Marinade

- ¼ cup + 2 tbsp of hot sauce
- ½ tsp of garlic powder

- ½ tsp of salt
- ½ tsp of black pepper
- ½ tsp of onion powder
- ¼ tsp of celery seed - OPTIONAL

Ginger Chicken Marinade

- ½ cup of soy sauce
- ¼ cup of sugar
- 1 tbsp of minced fresh ginger
- 1 whole garlic clove, minced
- ½ tsp of ground ginger
- ½ tsp of salt

Teriyaki Chicken Marinade

- ¾ cup of molasses
- ¾ cup of soy sauce
- ¾ cup of teriyaki sauce
- 6 tbsp of rock salt
- 1 tsp of onion powder
- 1 tsp of garlic powder
- 1 tsp of salt
- ¼ tsp of pepper

Lemon Rosemary Chicken Marinade

- 1 whole chopped orange

- 1 whole chopped lemon
- 2 cups of warm water
- 2 tsp of rosemary

Hot Pepper Chicken Marinade

- 2 ¼ tsp of pickling salt
- 2 ¼ tsp of tenderizing salt
- 1 tsp of crushed red pepper flakes
- ½ tsp of cayenne pepper
- ¼ tsp of white pepper
- ¼ tsp of black pepper
- 1/8 tsp of garlic powder
- 1/8 tsp of onion powder

Smoked Chicken Marinade

- 2 tbsp of Worcestershire sauce
- 2 tbsp of gourmet sauce
- 1 tbsp of brown sugar
- 1 tbsp of minced fresh ginger
- 2 whole garlic cloves, minced
- 1 tbsp of salt
- 1 tsp of paprika
- ¼ tsp of onion powder
- ¼ tsp of crushed red pepper flakes

Cajun Chicken Marinade

- 2 ¼ tsp of tenderizing salt
- 2 ¼ tsp of pickling salt
- 1 ¼ tsp of Cajun seasoning
- ¼ tsp of cayenne pepper
- 1/8 tsp of garlic powder
- 1/8 tsp of onion powder

Turkey

Basic Turkey Marinade

- ½ cup of water
- ¼ cup of soy sauce
- 2 tbsp of brown sugar
- 2 tsp of Worcestershire sauce
- 1 tsp of black pepper
- ½ tsp of onion powder
- ½ tsp of garlic powder

Spicy Turkey Marinade

- ¾ cup of soy sauce
- 3 tbsp of honey
- 2 tbsp of garlic-chili paste
- 2 tbsp of dried red chili flakes

Smoked Turkey Marinade

- ½ cup of soy sauce
- ¼ cup of water
- 2 tbsp of honey
- 2 tbsp of lime juice
- 1 tbsp of quick curing salt
- 1 to 2 tbsp of Asian garlic-chili paste

Jamaican Turkey Marinade

- 4 tbsp of soy sauce
- 1 tsp of lime juice
- 1 tsp of lemon juice
- 1 tsp of brown sugar
- ½ tsp of black pepper
- ½ tsp of cayenne pepper
- ¼ tsp of ground allspice
- ¼ tsp of garlic powder

Cilantro Lemon-Garlic Turkey Marinade

- Juice from 1 ½ lemons
- ¾ cup of chopped fresh cilantro
- ½ cup of soy sauce
- ½ cup of Worcestershire sauce
- 5 minced garlic cloves

- ½ tsp of onion powder

Ginger Teriyaki Turkey Marinade

- 1 cup of teriyaki sauce
- 2 ½ tbsp of brown sugar
- 2 tbsp of peeled, minced fresh ginger
- 1 tbsp of roasted sesame seeds
- 1 tbsp of sesame oil
- ½ tbsp of garlic powder

Sweet Maple Turkey Marinade

- ¼ cup of tamarin sauce or soy sauce
- 2 tbsp of maple syrup or maple sugar
- 2 tbsp of Worcestershire sauce
- 2 whole garlic cloves
- 1 ½ tsp of salt
- 1 ¼ tsp of pepper
- ½ tsp of cayenne pepper

Sweet and Spicy Venison Marinade

- ½ cup of Worcestershire sauce
- ½ cup of brown sugar
- ½ cup of teriyaki sauce
- 1/3 cup of soy sauce
- 3 tbsp of liquid smoke

- 1 tbsp of lemon juice
- 1 tbsp of garlic salt
- 1 tbsp of onion powder
- 1 tbsp of ground black pepper
- 1 tsp of paprika
- 1 tsp of hot pepper sauce

Wild Elk Marinade

- 4 tbsp of soy sauce
- 4 tbsp of Worcestershire sauce
- 1 tbsp of ketchup
- 1 to 2 minced garlic cloves
- ¾ tsp of kosher salt
- ¼ tsp of black pepper
- ¼ tsp of onion powder
- Red pepper flakes– OPTIONAL

Smoked Quail Marinade

- 2 cups of soy sauce
- 1 cup of red wine
- 1 cup of water
- 1/3 cup of sugar
- ¼ cup of salt – non-iodized
- ½ tsp of Tabasco sauce
- ½ tsp of garlic powder

- ½ tsp of onion powder
- ½ tsp of pepper

Reindeer Jerky Marinade

- ¾ cup of soy sauce
- 1 tbsp of brown sugar
- 1 tsp of liquid smoke
- 1 tsp of salt
- ½ tsp of pepper
- ½ tsp of grated fresh ginger
- ½ tsp of minced fresh garlic

Teriyaki Game Marinade

- 1 cup of teriyaki sauce
- ½ cup of water
- ½ cup of brown sugar
- 1/3 cup of soy sauce
- 1 tbsp of garlic powder
- 1 tbsp of onion powder
- 1 tbsp of black pepper
- 1 tbsp of liquid smoke

Wisconsin Style Game Marinade

- ¼ cup of soy sauce
- 1 tbsp of Worcestershire sauce

- 1 tbsp of steak sauce
- 1 tbsp of liquid smoke
- ½ tsp of sea salt
- ½ tsp of onion powder
- ½ tsp of fresh ground black pepper
- ½ tsp of garlic powder

Heat-Infused Barbecue Deer Marinade

- ½ cup of barbecue sauce
- ½ cup of Worcestershire sauce
- ¼ cup of chili sauce
- ¼ cup of maple syrup
- ¼ cup of hot sauce
- ¼ cup of sweet soy sauce
- ¼ cup of brown sugar
- 2 tbsp of minced fresh garlic
- 2 tbsp of chili powder
- 1 tbsp of liquid smoke
- 1 tbsp of pickled jalapeno pepper
- 1 tsp of sea salt
- 1 tsp of pepper

Fish

Trout Fish Marinade

- ¼ cup of soy sauce
- 1 tbsp of brown sugar
- 1 tsp of minced garlic
- 1 tsp of olive oil
- ½ tsp of ground black pepper

Hawaiian Fish Marinade

- ½ cup of soy sauce
- ¼ cup of pineapple juice
- 1 tbsp of brown sugar
- 1 tbsp of minced fresh ginger
- 1 minced garlic clove
- 1 tsp of salt
- 1 tsp of pepper
- ¼ tsp of cayenne pepper

Teriyaki Tuna Marinade

- ¾ cup of teriyaki sauce
- ½ cup of soy sauce
- 4 tbsp of sugar
- 2 tsp of grated fresh ginger
- 1 minced garlic clove

Spicy Salmon Marinade

- 1 cup of soy sauce
- 2 tbsp of molasses
- 2 tbsp of white sugar
- 2 tbsp of Worcestershire sauce
- 2 tbsp of lemon juice
- 1 ½ tbsp of black pepper
- 2 tsp of liquid smoke
- 1 ½ tsp of Tabasco

Lemon Pepper Fish Marinade

- ¼ cup of soy sauce
- ¼ cup of water
- 1 tsp of black pepper
- ½ tsp of garlic powder
- ½ tsp of salt
- ½ tsp of lemon pepper

Tangy Salmon Marinade

- ½ cup of water
- ½ cup of apple cider vinegar
- ½ cup of lemon juice
- 2 tbsp of coconut aminos
- 2 tsp of garlic powder

- 2 tsp of onion powder
- 1 tsp of salt

Korean Style Fish Marinade

- 3 tbsp of rice wine vinegar
- 2 to 3 tbsp of red chili paste
- 2 tbsp of mayonnaise
- 1 tbsp of soy sauce
- 1 tbsp of corn syrup
- 1 tbsp of sugar
- Sesame seeds for garnish

Other Recipes
Rabbit Marinade

- 2/3 cup of soy sauce
- ½ cup of pineapple juice
- ½ cup of brown sugar
- 1/3 cup of balsamic vinegar
- ¼ cup of Worcestershire sauce
- ¼ cup of teriyaki sauce
- 5 tbsp of liquid smoke
- 1 tbsp of garlic powder
- 1 tbsp of onion powder
- 2 tsp of pepper

- 1 tsp of red pepper flakes

Sweet Alligator Marinade

- 1 cup of curing salt
- 2 quarts of water
- ½ cup of brown sugar or molasses
- 4 tbsp of pepper
- 1 tsp of garlic puree

Duck or Goose Marinade

- 2 cups of water
- ¼ cup of Worcestershire sauce
- 3 tbsp of brown sugar
- 2 tbsp of kosher salt
- 1 tsp of garlic powder
- 1 tsp of cayenne
- 1 tsp of dried thyme
- 1 tsp of porcini powder

Lamb Marinade

- ¼ cup of Worcestershire sauce
- ¼ cup of soy sauce
- 1 tsp of garlic powder
- 1 tsp of ground black pepper
- 1 tsp of onion powder

- ½ tsp of chili powder
- ½ tsp of salt
- ¼ tsp of celery seed

Goat Marinade

- ½ cup of Worcestershire sauce
- ½ cup of teriyaki sauce
- 2 tbsp of black pepper
- 1 tbsp of seasoning salt
- 1 tbsp of liquid smoke

Bear Marinade

- 1 quart of water
- ½ cup of brown sugar
- ¼ cup of curing salt
- 1 tbsp of garlic granules
- 1 tbsp of black pepper

Honey Glazed Pork Marinade

- 2 tbsp of honey
- 2 tbsp of fish sauce
- 2 tbsp of soy sauce
- 2 tbsp of dark soy sauce
- 2 tbsp of sugar
- 1 tbsp of cooking wine

- 1 tsp of five-spice powder
- ½ tsp of ground black pepper
- Cayenne pepper to taste

Ginger Pigeon Marinade

- 1 cup of soy sauce
- ½ cup of water
- ½ cup of maple syrup
- 1 tsp of grated fresh ginger
- 1 pinch of cayenne pepper

Spicy Bison Marinade

- 1 ½ cups of Worcestershire sauce
- 2 tbsp of chopped fresh garlic
- 2 tbsp of crushed red pepper flakes
- 1 tbsp of freshly cracked black pepper
- 1 tbsp of sugar
- 1 tsp of liquid smoke

Curing Jerky

Curing salt is sometimes added to jerky to give it a longer shelf life, make it taste better, and keep its color. While you don't need to add it to your jerky recipe, it is something you should consider. That's because curing salt inhibits bacteria that can cause foodborne illnesses.

This section will look into what curing salt is and how you use it with jerky, giving you all the information you need to decide whether to use it.

The Effect of Curing Salt

Traditional jerky cure is a mixture of food coloring, sodium chloride, and sodium nitrite, and its main functions are:

1. **To Enhance Flavor:** Think of jerky cure as being salt with impressive powers. It enhances the natural flavors of the meat and marinade, but you must be mindful of how you use it. Always follow the usage directions to the letter, as high levels can be toxic. As a rule, you only need a teaspoon for every five pounds of meat. You will also find that most curing salt is pink, created by adding food coloring, so you don't confuse it with normal table salt.

2. **It Retains the Jerky Color:** Because curing salt is an antioxidant, it helps the meat retain its color and stops it from fading, which usually happens when it is exposed to the air. When jerky has been cured, it looks fresh and vibrant.

3. **It Inhibits Bacteria:** Curing salt can stop bacteria from growing in the meat, which makes it a critical tool for beginner jerky makers.

Are Curing Salts for Jerky Safe?

Right now, there is nothing to say that curing salts are not safe to use. There have been plenty of academic and scientific studies on sodium nitrite, and they all say the same thing. When sodium nitrite is used at the right levels, it is effective and safe to use in preventing bacterial growth.

It must be said that there is some suspicion about curing salts, in particular sodium nitrite and nitrate. Just a few years ago, a report was released by the International Agency for Research on Cancer, stating that some human cancers may be caused by processed meat, particularly cured meat. However, there was no mention of the effect of meat or nitrates on overall health.,

It might surprise you to learn that many of the fruits and veggies you enjoy actually contain nitrates. According to a study published by the American Journal of Clinical Nutrition, around 80% of the nitrates in your diet come from vegetables.

When all is said and done, it is down to each person to consider the benefits and risks and decide whether to use curing salts. If you choose not to, there are some other alternatives. For example, there are natural nitrates in celery juice or powder and these have the same benefits as curing salt, especially in terms of function and flavor. When celery nitrates are introduced to specific bacteria, those nitrates turn into nitrites, offering characteristics similar to those of a jerky cure.

That said, natural cures are really not easy to work with because nitrate measurement can't be accurately measured. Not only that, but they are more expensive than curing salt and can be just as toxic in the wrong amounts.

The Difference between Cure #1 vs. Cure #2

Curing salt is sold under several names – pink salt, Instacure, Prague powder, etc. While they are interchangeable, it is important to get the right cure for what you are making. Two important designations are cure #1 and

#2. #1 has sodium nitrite and salt, while #2 has sodium nitrite, salt, and sodium nitrate.

Here are the differences between them and how to know when to use each one:

CURE	COMMON NAMES	INGREDIENTS	WHEN TO USE	EXAMPLE PRODUCTS
Cure #1	Instacure #1 Prague Powder #1	Salt Sodium nitrite	For foods needing 30 days or less to process.	Sausage Jerky Pastrami Bacon Hot dog Ham Corned beef
Cure #2	Instacure #2 Prague Powder #2	Salt Sodium Nitrite Sodium Nitrate	For foods needing more than 30 days to process	Prosciutto Salami Pepperoni

How to Store Curing Salt

Curing salt should be stored somewhere cool and dry, away from any light source. It should also be kept from moisture to ensure it stays fresh for longer. If kept properly, it can last for a long time. Make sure you label it clearly so you don't get it confused with other salts and use it incorrectly.

Where to Buy Curing Salt

Curing salt can be found online. Just look for retailers selling seasonings, herbs, and spices, or stores selling meat processing paraphernalia or sporting stores. So long as you buy it from a reputable source, it should be of the best quality. A one-pound bag of cure will last for hundreds of pounds of meat, as you only need one teaspoon per five pounds.

Chapter 7: Storing and Packaging Jerky

Jerky was invented to preserve food, specifically protein, for times when little food was available. It's easy enough to make – the meat or fish must be dried at low temperatures over a long period of time to remove the moisture, enabling it to be stored for a long period. And that is one of the biggest questions: how long can you store jerky?

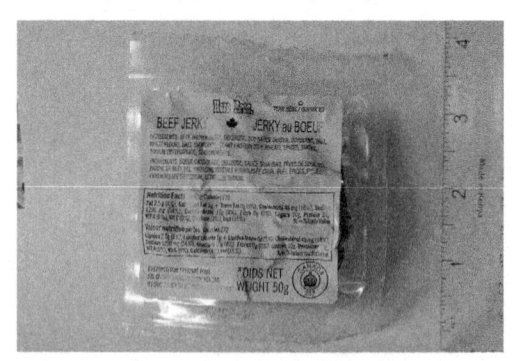

19. Jerky can be sealed in bags to keep it from being spoiled. Source: Dvermeirre, CC BY-SA 4.0 <https://creativecommons.org/licenses/by-sa/4.0>, via Wikimedia Commons: https://commons.wikimedia.org/wiki/File:IMP_Jerky_Front.JPG

The following tips will ensure that your jerky can be stored for up to two months, provided you package it right. However, if you put it in the pantry in a Ziploc bag, it will only last a week, or up to two weeks in the refrigerator. You'll also learn about the signs of spoiled jerky and how to stop it from happening.

How to Make Jerky Last Longer

Certain things impact the shelf life of your jerky, and there are certain things you should do to make that time longer:

1. **Use Lean Meat:** Fat is not good for jerky as it spoils the meat faster and will go rancid.

2. **Use Curing Salt:** Salt stops bacteria from growing in meat that may be exposed to oxygen. You'll note that many recipes don't include salt, so the meat has to be heated to 160°F inside (165°F for fish and poultry), and table or pickling salt is used to keep the bacteria away. However, you can use curing salt instead.

3. **Drying Time:** The longer your jerky is left to dry, the longer it will last. However, there is a fine line because over-drying will give you a tough product. Dry it to the consistency you want, and then ensure you package it properly to lengthen the shelf life – that will be discussed shortly.

4. **Storage:** When jerky is made on a commercial scale, the oxygen is removed at the time of packaging, which is why it stays fresh for much longer. This is done using a process where the packages have nitrogen pushed into them, which then pushes out all the oxygen. However, it's highly unlikely that you will have nitrogen lying around your house, so you'll need

to follow the steps below to make sure your jerky can last for as long as possible:

- **Cool It Off:** Your jerky should be cold before being stored. If it is even a little warm, it lets off moisture.

- **Paper Bags:** Store the jerky in paper bags for a few days. This will remove any excess moisture before you vacuum-seal or store it in airtight containers.

- **Mason Jars and Ziploc Bags:** These are both airtight packaging options, making them an excellent choice. Do not leave your jars or bags in direct sunlight, though, as they will sweat.

- **Oxygen Absorbers:** You can buy these fairly cheaply and place them in your storage container or packaging. They help extend the life of your jerky by absorbing oxygen and stopping bacteria from growing.

- **Vacuum Sealers:** When you vacuum-seal your jerky, oxygen cannot get to it, thus extending its shelf-life. Vacuum sealers are inexpensive and are perfect for making snack packages of jerky.

- **Pantry:** Store your packaging in dark, cool places, like your pantry. It must never be left in sunlight as condensation will form in the package, making your jerky moldy. If drops of water appear after you have stored the jerky, it wasn't dry enough. Take it out and run it through the drying process again.

- **Fridge:** Jerky can be safely stored for about a month in the refrigerator but you should let it come back to room temperature before you eat it. That way, it won't be so hard.
- **Freezer:** Jerky will freeze well for up to six months. However, it can change the taste, so it should only be done if you have no other way. Instead, make smaller batches more often.

After opening homemade jerky, you should consume it within three to five days or up to a week if you store it in the refrigerator.

Looking for Spoilage

There are two ways to tell if your jerky has gone bad – smell and mold. If your jerky doesn't smell right, ditch it. It's not worth the risk of eating it.

Mold shows up as a white, fuzzy substance on the outside of the jerky, and if you see it on one piece, the whole bag must be thrown. That's because it's highly likely the rest also has mold spores on it, and eating it can lead to food poisoning.

What causes mold to appear on your jerky?

The main reasons are that there is too much moisture, which means you didn't dry it properly, and too much oxygen, which means you didn't package it properly. Both will cause bacteria to grow on the jerky and lead to mold forming.

When you dry your jerky, you must remove 90 to 95% of the moisture. The American Medical Association published a report stating that E. coli can survive in meat at temperatures of up to 145°F and up to 10 hours during drying. This is why meat should really be precooked until it has an internal temperature of 165°F unless drying at a temperature of 160°F for several hours.

Main Causes of Food Spoilage

Understanding how food spoilage happens is key to understanding how to package the jerky.

- **Microorganisms**

There are two types of microorganisms you need to be concerned about, spoilage and pathogenic. The latter can cause food-borne illnesses, such as listeria, E. coli, and salmonella. The only way to stop these from occurring is to make sure the meat is cooked at the right temperature and time the recipe states or to precook it first. If you do that, these pathogenic microorganisms will not be an issue.

In terms of spoilage, yeast, bacteria, and mold are the important ones you need to eliminate and tend to occur if the meat is not handled or stored properly after drying.

- **Air**

Oxidation can change how your jerky looks and tastes and impacts its nutritional density. When your jerky is exposed to air for too long, it loses its color and flavor and dries out. One result of this is rancidity, which is when the fat in the meat goes off, which is why lean meat is essential when making jerky.

- **Light**

Extended exposure to light can also have the same effects as air exposure, specifically changing the color and drying it out. It can also raise the temperature, shortening the shelf life, and hastening the speed at which the jerky goes off.

- **Temperature**

At higher temperatures, food goes off much quicker, and temperature fluctuations can also cause sweating on the jerky, little beads of moisture that quickly cause mold to grow.

- **Insects, Rodents, and Other Pests**

Pests, like rodents and some insects, love jerky, and they can cause damage to the packaging that lets in light, moisture, and air. And let's not forget that many of these pests carry bacteria that can potentially harm you.

The Importance of Packaging

First, a story.

Let's say that you've finally perfected your jerky. You've got the right texture and a wonderful flavor and made a ton of it. But you don't have enough airtight containers to store it in.

What do you do? You shove it in a Ziploc bag, do it up, and put it in the refrigerator. A week later, your jerky is off and has a weird texture. Why?

Because of the packaging.

While Ziploc bags are fine for storing jerky, they are only good if you can get rid of all the oxygen. Jerky is highly perishable and must be kept vacuum-packed or in another airtight container.

Here are some of the best ways to package your jerky to extend its shelf life:

- **Plastic Bags:** This might seem obvious, but it's also one of the best choices, so long as you can remove the oxygen. Stored properly, jerky packaged in plastic will retain its moisture, texture, color, and flavor. You can write the date on the bag so you know when it was stored. However, one drawback is that pests can easily attack plastic, so when you place your jerky in plastic bags, place it inside another glass or plastic container that you can seal. Use food-grade bags intended for freezer use, as these are tougher and last longer.

- **Mason Jars:** The lid on a mason jar creates an airtight seal, although your jerky will still spoil faster than if it were in a plastic bag. That's because opening the jar, allowing air in, and removing it again is not easy. Glass jars offer better protection against pests.

- **Plastic Containers:** Like the Mason jars, these are airtight when the lid is sealed on correctly. However, they do let air in when the lid is opened and this can shorten the shelf life considerably.

- **Vacuum Sealed Bags:** These are a good storage option for storing large amounts of jerky long-term. In fact, sealed properly, the jerky will last up to two years if not opened. However, the vacuum sealing process can squeeze flavor and fat from the jerky, so it doesn't do much for the texture. If you want to vacuum-pack your jerky, do it in small amounts you know won't be stored for long.

In short, your jerky needs to be packaged in something that offers barrier protection against everything that can negatively affect it. The best way is to use plastic bags with the oxygen removed and then store it inside plastic or glass containers in a dark, cool place. Alternatively, store it in the refrigerator if you intend to eat it fairly quickly.

Chapter 8: Exploring Jerky Culture and Innovations

Jerky was once a way to preserve food over the long term, designed to help feed people in times of famine or low food supplies. Now, it is one of the most popular high-protein snacks, especially for athletes and hikers, and it's come a long way since it was invented. In the final chapter, you will learn its cultural significance and some innovations that have led to jerky attaining its status.

20. Kilishi is a popular form of jerky. Source: Aderiqueza, CC BY-SA 4.0 <https://creativecommons.org/licenses/by-sa/4.0>, via Wikimedia Commons: https://commons.wikimedia.org/wiki/File:Kilishi_(Beef_Jerky).jpg

The Cultural Significance of Jerky

Jerky's origins go back many thousands of years to ancient civilizations, and it means something different to each culture. Jerky isn't seen as just a food source anymore. Instead, it is a sign of tradition and indicates just how resourceful your ancestors were in storing food.

While most Americans believe that jerky is theirs and theirs alone, most countries have their own jerky traditions. There isn't anything difficult about it, but the fascinating part is how each country creates jerky and how they consume it. Here are some of the ways it is produced and eaten across the world:

China – Bak Kwa

Bak Kwa means "pork chip" and it is traditionally prepared at Chinese New Year. It is a salty, sweet jerky made from pigs or sometimes cows. It is marinated in fish sauce, five-spice powder, soy sauce, sugar, salt, sesame oil, and ground black pepper and left to dry at 122°F to 140°F.

Bak Kwa is darker and more hardened than other jerkies because of the slightly higher temperatures. However, these days, the recipe has been modified to cook it at a lower temperature for a softer texture, and some also leave the sugar out. In fact, Bak Kwa now has a huge diversity in its textures and flavors, making it one of the most popular snacks across China.

As people began to migrate from China to Singapore and Malaysia, they took their recipes with them, and it didn't take long for their cultures to start adapting them. Malaysian Bak Kwa is smoked over charcoal, giving it a full-bodied, rich flavor. They also created a spicy chili version of Bak Kwa.

Nigeria – Kilishi

This is created by drying Suya, a popular dish in Africa, and it is similar to a kebab, given that it is marinated, grilled meat on a skewer. However, the difference is that although both dishes are made from beef, sheep, or goat, kilishi meat is sliced much thinner and dried, not grilled.

Kilishi is marinated in Dobu (a peanut sauce made in Nigeria,) spices, water, ground onions, and salt, and the sweetness is added with date palms or honey. It is precooked and then left to dry for several hours.

Kilishi combines spicy and sweet, and many Nigerians eat it topped off with more pepper. What sets kilishi aside from other jerkies is that it can last for nearly six months without any changes to its texture or flavor, and this is likely why it was the preferred food source for migrating tribes.

Spain – Cecina

Cecina is similar to Prosciutto in texture and flavor but is drier. Traditionally eaten as an appetizer in parts of Spain, it originated in a historic Northern Spain city called Leon. It is traditionally made from meat shaved from a cow's hind legs, although early recipes indicate that horse and rabbit meat were also used.

Cecina is simple to make. The meat is shaved, salted, and dried for several days – air, sun, or smoked – until the right flavor and texture are achieved. It is a smoky, crispy jerky with sweet undertones and is usually drizzled with olive oil and served with Manzanilla olives and Manchego cheese.

India – Uppu Kandam

Uppu Kandam is a traditional part of Indian cuisine that originated in Tamil Nadu. Dried in the sun, dishes like this are delicacies in this southern Indian city because their preparation takes a long time. That's why it is normally reserved for special occasions, such as ceremonies and religious holidays.

Usually, it is made from thinly sliced goat mutton, rubbed with turmeric, salt, pepper, and chili powder, and left in the sun to dry. However, unlike many jerkies that are eaten as snacks or appetizers, Uppu Kandam is an ingredient and is typically added to curries and gravies to give them a savory, salty kick. It does have a long shelf life, though, almost six months.

Italy – Coppiette

Translated as "little couples," Coppiette is a type of hard salami that originated in Lazio. Typically eaten as an appetizer, it was once the food of poorer farmers, made as a way to make their livestock meat go further.

These days, it is made from pork, but in its early days, butchers would use the hind legs of horses, donkeys, goats, and sheep. It starts the same as any jerky, seasoned with spicy pepper and fennel seeds. It is then cured, sliced into the thin, long strips we see today, and dried in pairs. It has a savory, aromatic flavor with a chewy texture.

Modern Culinary Trends and Innovations

These days, more and more people are trying to add more protein to their diets, and one of the easiest ways to do that is to eat jerky. Now one of the most popular snacks in the world, the global market has really taken off. Not only is jerky convenient, but it also suits most diets and comes in plenty of different flavors and textures.

These are two of the more common trends and innovations we see today:

1. **Interesting Flavors:** These days, you can buy jerky in just about any flavor you can think of, including pineapple-habanero, ginger-teriyaki, maple-hickory-bacon, and sweet cherry, to name just a few.

2. **Plant-Based**: It's fair to say that plant-based foods have grown in popularity considerably over the last few years. If you can eat something in its natural meat form, you can get a plant-based version, too. Lots of people choose to be vegan but still want to enjoy jerky. Now, you can buy or make vegan jerky from beans, nuts, flax, seaweed, coconut, tofu, and, of course, dried veggies, like beets, carrots, mushrooms, and so on.

Jerky Pairings

While jerky is great to eat on its own, it also goes really well with different food and drinks. Some of the best pairings are:

- **Jerky and Cheese:** Meat and cheese is one of the most common pairings, no matter the occasion. Instead of pairing cheese with salami or sausage, use jerky instead, and try different flavor combinations – Havarti cheese with cherry maple jerky or Gouda cheese with smoky jerky, for example.

- **Jerky and Salad:** Most people add some form of protein to their salads, so instead of using chicken or ham, add different flavored jerky instead.

- **Jerky and Beer:** Wings and beer go together, and so do jerky and beer. Think about the flavor profiles – a dry stout pairs well with barbecue jerky, while an IPA works well with spicy jerky, and golden ales pair well with teriyaki.

Why Jerky Is More Popular Than Ever

As a snack, jerky has long been ingrained in worldwide cultures. Once a means to survival, it is now eaten as a snack by people everywhere. Every year, the industry ups its game, developing new products to meet new preferences, and it is now more popular than ever before. Why? Here's why:

1. **It's a Classic Snack:** First appearing in human history in about 1550 BC, jerky was likely developed by a South American Inca tribe called the Quechua. They called it "charqui," which means "dried meat." From there, it evolved and became truly popular in North America during the Cowboy era. It could be stored for months and offered a great protein source when other food sources were low during the winter. Today, it is a classic snack, often eaten by hikers and campers to keep them going.

2. **More Variety:** While traditional jerky is chewy, tough, and smoky, today, there are many more varieties available and not just made from beef. You can now buy or make jerky from buffalo, alligator, crocodile, kangaroo, ostrich, and many other animals. But that's not where the variety stops. Different ingredients are added to change the flavor profiles, including sweet onion, hot and sweet, pineapple, honey BBQ, cherry-maple jalapeno, and many more.

3. **Better Quality:** Commercial manufacturers tend to focus on producing large quantities of traditional jerky. However, smaller companies don't just focus on different meat and flavoring. They also focus on

ingredients and processing quality. Now, fresh animals and the highest quality seasonings and spices are used. Many producers now only use animals free from steroids, hormones, and antibiotics, free-range animals that lead a healthy natural life. This has brought in a whole new batch of customers who put ethics above all else.

4. **Versatility:** Jerky is undoubtedly incredibly versatile. You can carry it with you wherever you go, and it serves as one of the most protein-rich, eat-on-the-go snacks. Carry it in your pocket wherever you go, knowing it won't go off quickly. You can even add it to soups, to a cheese or charcuterie board, chopped into salads, and many more.

5. **The Prepping Age:** Prepping is becoming mainstream, especially in light of the recent pandemic and the current wars across the world. Jerky is a great product to add to a prepper's pantry, as it takes little room and can be made and stored in large quantities. It provides much-needed protein, doesn't need to be reheated, and is the best all-round choice for preppers everywhere.

6. **It's Healthy:** When you make your own marinades, you control the ingredients, which is better than buying store-made marinades packed with preservatives and other unhealthy ingredients.

When you grill or broil meat at high temperatures, carcinogenic compounds can form in the meat, which is why eating too much meat is said to contribute to some cancers. Marinades prevent these compounds from forming. Some of the many health benefits that jerky offers are:

- **Low-Carb**: If you have chosen a low-carb lifestyle or you can't eat gluten, finding the right snacks is hard. Jerky is the ultimate snack, packed with protein, filling, and it tastes fantastic.

- **It Contains Iron**: One of the best sources of natural iron is red meat, and jerky offers a high percentage of what you need every day.

- **Low Fat**: When you make jerky, you use lean meat, and cut off as much fat as you can. Any internal fat in the meat usually disappears as the meat dries.

- **A Great Protein Source**: Every slice of jerky is packed with protein, providing a high percentage of your daily needs. For example, an egg and a slice of jerky each provide 12% of your daily protein needs. The jerky is half the weight of the egg, which means each ounce provides twice the protein the egg does.

- **Boosts Immunity**: Beef jerky offers a decent amount of zinc per slice, a critical mineral for a healthy immune system.

- **Boosts Energy**: The high iron level provides energy levels with a much-needed boost. Your body needs iron to move oxygen to where it needs to go. As the human body is not capable of making iron, you need to get it from your food, and jerky made from red meat is a great source.

- **Improves Heart Health**: As well as iron and zinc, jerky also provides potassium, which is vital for helping the blood move through your arteries to improve heart muscle stimulation. In this way, it helps regulate your heart rate and blood pressure.

- **Improves Cholesterol**: Jerky is packed with high levels of dietary fiber, which improves cholesterol levels. This works because the fiber binds to the molecules of cholesterol in your blood and takes it out of your body. This results in lower levels of low-density lipoproteins, or LDL – the "bad" cholesterol.

- **Improves Your Bone Health**: Lastly, red meat jerky also offers a good level of phosphorus, which is needed to keep your teeth and bones healthy. It is a common misconception that you only need calcium for teeth and bones, when in fact, the calcium can't do it without phosphorus. Phosphorus also levels your blood pH and helps fat, carbs, and protein turn into energy.

7. **It's Fun to Make:** While you can grab a bag of jerky at your local grocery store, the fun part about it is that you can also make it in your own home. It isn't difficult, and you can create some amazing flavor profiles if you just let your creative side out.

Finding Your Inspiration

Following jerky recipes is fun for a while, but it soon becomes boring when you find you are always producing the same old flavors of jerky. The trick to making jerky is to get creative, not just with flavors but also with textures.

Here are some ideas to find your jerky inspiration:

1. **Jot Your Ideas Down:** No matter where you are, have a notebook and pen to hand, even in bed at night. When an idea strikes you, you should write it down. Ideas will always come to you when you least expect them, and the only way to remember them is to write them down. You don't have to use pen and paper. If you want, you can use the Notes facility on your phone, so long as you jot them down and remember them. That way, you have them to hand whenever you want to try a new recipe.

2. **Research and Experiment:** The more you make jerky and the more you create your own recipes, the easier you'll find it to learn the best flavors to go together. For example, you know that peanut butter and chocolate go together, but in terms of jerky, what about mango and salmon? Or pineapple and smoky bacon? Experimenting is the only way to truly understand what works together and what doesn't. Once you understand flavor pairings, you can create some of the most amazing ideas.

3. **Use Pinterest:** Pinterest is packed with ideas for recipes, and it's one of the best places to find inspiration. Run a search for "jerky flavors" and see what comes up. Take your inspiration from the recipes you find, but don't copy them. Use their ideas, but add your own unique spin to it.

4. **Think about In-Season or Trending Foods:** This is more true if you are making plant-based jerky, as you can use in-season fruits and veggies. But you should also think about trending flavors and try to use those in your marinades to give your jerky an in-

season, trendy flavor everyone will love. Head to the local farmer's market to see what's on offer, and don't forget to consider holidays and celebrations coming up – you can get a lot of inspiration from that.

5. **Get Your Inspiration from What Doesn't Work:** That might sound odd, but bad ideas can sometimes lead to good ones. When something clearly doesn't work, stop trying to make it work. Take a step back, look at it, and figure out where you can tweak it. If you do the work, the rewards will come. Figure out what didn't work, and do one of three things: forget about it, change it, or have another go later. Write down a list of every recipe that doesn't work and look over it – sometimes, a truly excellent idea will jump out at you!

6. **Challenge Yourself:** Turn your jerky-making into a challenge. Don't be scared to experiment, but do it with small batches of jerky. That way, if your experiment doesn't work, it's not too much of a loss. Here's how to do it. Think of a different ingredient – a meat or fish you haven't worked with before, a different spice, vegetable, protein source, etc. - and create jerky with it. You might just surprise yourself with what you end up creating. It might be a complete disaster, in which case you should move on and forget you ever made it, or it could be something completely fantastic. In that case, you could even experiment and see if you can make it even better. Do this every month or even weekly, just to get your creative juices flowing again and expand your skills while you are at it.

Conclusion

Thank you for reading *"Jerky Recipes: The Ultimate Guide to Drying and Preserving Meat, Fish, Fowl, and More through Traditional Methods."* Hopefully, you have learned everything you need to know about making jerky and can see that it isn't as difficult as you might have thought it was.

Here's what you learned.

In Chapter 1, you read about the history of jerky and its significance in history, while Chapter 2 discussed the ingredients. You learned how to choose the right cut of meat, a little bit about seasoning and marinating your meat for different flavor profiles, and how to source your ingredients.

In Chapter 3, you learned how to prepare your meat to turn it into jerky, several drying methods, and how marinading and curing impact the flavor. Chapter 4 discussed how to dehydrate and smoke jerky, offering plenty of tips to help you get it right. You also learned about texture and consistency.

Chapter 5 gave you a ton of recipes for making all different kinds of jerky – beef, chicken, fish, goose, game, and even a selection of vegan and vegetarian options, while

Chapter 6 discussed seasoning and marinading, providing you with plenty of recipes to help you make your own flavor profiles, and also discussed curing.

Chapter 7 looked at how and why you should package jerky and how to store it for maximum freshness and shelf life, while Chapter 8 discussed the cultural significance of jerky and some of the many innovations in preparation and flavor profiles that have evolved over the years.

Thank you once again for reading this book. If you enjoyed it, please consider leaving a review to help others.

Lastly, have fun in your new venture, expand your jerky-making knowledge, and bring your creative side out to play – there really is no limit to what you can do.

References

4 Health Benefits of Beef Jerky (And It's Not Just the Protein!). (n.d.). Top Notch Jerky. https://www.topnotchjerky.com/blogs/info/health-benefits-of-beef-jerky

5 Different Methods for Drying Jerky. (n.d.). The Spruce Eats. https://www.thespruceeats.com/jerky-drying-methods-1808216

8 Reasons Why Jerky Is More Popular Than Ever. (2022, June 14). Lee's Market Jerky. https://www.leesmarketjerky.com/blogs/news/8-reasons-why-jerky-is-more-popular-than-ever

Backcountry Paleo /. (2014, September 1). Gobble Up Some Turkey Jerky! Backcountry Paleo. https://www.backcountrypaleo.com/gobble-up-some-turkey-jerky/

bbjadmin. (2020, August 25). The Best Cuts of Meat to Use When Making Jerky. BULK BEEF JERKY. https://www.bulkbeefjerky.com.au/the-best-cuts-of-meat-to-use-when-making-jerky/

Beef Jerky Increasing in Popularity and Flavor Trends. (2020, May 7). Advanced Biotech. https://adv-bio.com/beef-jerky-increasing-in-popularity-and-flavor-trends/

Beef Jerky Recipes. (2015, March 2). Jerkyholic. https://www.jerkyholic.com/beef-jerky-recipes/#recipes-test+wprm_type:beef-jerky

Best Cuts of Meat for Beef Jerky | Ultimate Guide. (2023, February 4). People's Choice Beef Jerky.

https://peopleschoicebeefjerky.com/blogs/news/best-meat-for-beef-jerky#:~:text=The%20selection%20of%20a%20cut

Best Fish Jerky: Taste the Difference of Our Grade-A Wild Coho Salmon Jerky! (n.d.). Mahogany Smoked Meats. https://smokedmeats.com/blogs/news/best-fish-jerky

BondBlogger, S., & Chef », food creator M. dream M. F. T. (2022, January 22). Air Fryer Chicken Jerky Recipe. Magic Skillet. https://magicskillet.com/recipe/air-fryer-chicken-jerky-recipe/?utm_campaign=yummly&utm_medium=yummly&utm_source=yummly

Campaigns, T. M. (2021, October 11). 7 Vegetarian Jerky Options Better Than Beef. The Monday Campaigns. https://www.mondaycampaigns.org/meatless-monday/7-vegetarian-jerky-options-better-than-beef

Chicken Jerky. (2021, April 8). Jerkyholic. https://www.jerkyholic.com/chicken-jerky/

Deer Jerky. (n.d.). Allrecipes. https://www.allrecipes.com/recipe/46324/deer-jerky/

Duck or Goose Breast Jerky | Traeger Grills. (n.d.). Https://Www.traeger.com. https://www.traeger.com/recipes/duck-breast-jerky

Everything You Need to Know about Jerky Drying Methods. (n.d.). Carnivore Club USA. https://us.carnivoreclub.co/blogs/the-daily-meat/everything-you-need-to-know-about-jerky-drying-methods

Hansen, S. (2022, April 13). 13 Pro Tips on How to Make Jerky in a Smoker. BBQ CHAMPS. https://bbqchamps.com/how-to-make-jerky/

How Long to Marinate Jerky? Not What You Think. (2023, January 30). People's Choice Beef Jerky. https://peopleschoicebeefjerky.com/blogs/news/how-long-to-marinate-jerky#:~:text=The%20marination%20of%20beef%20jerky

How to Make a Juicy Rabbit Jerky: Things You Need to Know (2020, January 16). Onthegas.org. https://onthegas.org/food/rabbit-jerky/

How to Make Dried Meat by Microwave Meat Dryer Machine. (2020, September 12). Industrial Food Drying Machines for Sale. https://food-drying-machine.com/food-drying-solution/how-to-make-dried-meat.html

How to Make Fish Jerky in a Dehydrator, Smoker, Oven, and More. (n.d.). Mahogany Smoked Meats. https://smokedmeats.com/blogs/news/how-to-make-fish-jerky

How to Make Trout Fish Jerky. (n.d.). The Spruce Eats. https://www.thespruceeats.com/trout-jerky-recipe-1808980

How to Slice Meat for Jerky [5 Steps with Photos]. (2023, January 30). People's Choice Beef Jerky. https://peopleschoicebeefjerky.com/blogs/news/how-to-slice-meat-for-jerky

How to Store Homemade Jerky [Professional Secrets]. (2023, February 1). People's Choice Beef Jerky. https://peopleschoicebeefjerky.com/blogs/news/how-to-store-homemade-jerky

How to Store Jerky: Short Term & Long Term. (n.d.). PackFreshUSA. https://packfreshusa.com/blog/how-to-store-jerky-short-term-long-term/

Great British Chefs (n.d.). Salmon Jerky Recipe - Great British Chefs. Www.greatbritishchefs.com. https://www.greatbritishchefs.com/recipes/salmon-jerky-recipe

Is Beef Jerky a Healthy Snack? Let's Find Out. (2022, July 27). HealthifyMe. https://www.healthifyme.com/blog/beef-jerky/

Make Beef Jerky in a Dehydrator [Step-by-Step Guide]. (2023, April 5). People's Choice Beef Jerky. https://peopleschoicebeefjerky.com/blogs/news/how-to-make-beef-jerky-in-a-dehydrator

Make Your Own Jerky. (n.d.). Three Jerks Jerky. https://www.threejerksjerky.com/pages/how-to-make-your-own-beef-jerky

Make Your Own Jerky & Recipes (n.d.). Smoking Gun Jerky. https://www.smokinggunjerky.com/recepies

Miles, J. (2013, February 22). Fish Recipe: Hawaiian Fish Jerky. Field & Stream. https://www.fieldandstream.com/blogs/wild-chef/2013/02/fish-recipe-hawaiian-fish-jerky/

MyNewsGH. (2023, November 27). The Cultural Significance of Jerky in Different Regions. MyNewsGh. https://www.mynewsgh.com/the-cultural-significance-of-jerky-in-different-regions/

Orange-Soy-Ginger Rabbit-Belly Jerky Recipe. (n.d.). Realtree Store. https://realtree.com/timber-2-table-wild-game-recipes/orange-soy-ginger-rabbit-belly-jerky-recipe

Relle. (2020, June 4). Sakura Boshi Recipe (Dried Fish Jerky). Keeping It Relle. https://keepingitrelle.com/sakura-boshi-recipe/

Segal, J. (2021, January 21). The Best Homemade Beef Jerky Recipe. Once upon a Chef. https://www.onceuponachef.com/recipes/the-best-homemade-beef-jerky-recipe.html

Shaw, H. (2012, February 29). Duck or Goose Jerky Recipe - How to Make Duck Jerky. Hunter Angler Gardener Cook. https://honest-food.net/duck-or-goose-jerky/

Shaw, H. (2013, April 22). A Chef's Guide: How to Make Venison Jerky. North American Whitetail. https://www.northamericanwhitetail.com/editorial/a-chefs-guide-how-to-make-venison-jerky/263139

Shea, M. R. (2020, October 3). Wild Game Jerky: The Ultimate Guide to Killer Meat. Free Range American. https://freerangeamerican.us/ultimate-jerky/

Smoky Chicken Jerky. (n.d.). Allrecipes. https://www.allrecipes.com/recipe/267889/smoky-chicken-jerky/

The Unbelievable & Wild History of Beef Jerky. (2015, November 9). People's Choice Beef Jerky. https://peopleschoicebeefjerky.com/blogs/news/history-of-beef-jerky

Top 3 Advantages of Flexible Packaging for Jerky - Pouch.me. (n.d.). https://pouch.me/top-3-advantages-of-flexible-packaging-for-jerky/

Unbelievably Delicious Honey-Miso Salmon Jerky Recipe. (2023, February 17). People's Choice Beef Jerky. https://peopleschoicebeefjerky.com/blogs/news/salmon-jerky-recipe

Wayne, D. (2022, April 10). Jalapeno Garlic Chicken Jerky in the Air Fryer. TheWildWaynes. https://thewildwaynes.com/jalapeno-garlic-chicken-jerky-in-the-air-fryer/#recipe

What Is Jerky? 10 Facts About Jerky - Raging Bull Snacks. (2023, February 20). Ragingbullsnacks.com. https://ragingbullsnacks.com/what-is-jerky-everything-you-need-to-know/

Will. (2021, March 29). The BEST Turkey Jerky Recipe. Jerkyholic. https://www.jerkyholic.com/turkey-jerky/#recipe

Woods, P. (n.d.). Fish Jerky Recipe in 6 Easy Steps - Dehydrator Spot. https://www.dehydratorspot.com/fish-jerky-recipe/

Printed in Great Britain
by Amazon